D1738024

A COLLOQUY ON CHRISTIAN EDUCATION

Contributors

JAMES D. ANDERSON (*chapter 23*) is assistant to the bishop for parish development, Diocese of Washington, Episcopal Church, Mount Saint Alban, Washington, D.C.

BOB BURT (*chapter 15*) is editor of youth publications and *Focus* magazine, Division of Christian Education, United Church Board for Homeland Ministries, Philadelphia, Pa.

FRANCES W. EASTMAN (*chapter 12*) is secretary for special program development, Division of Christian Education, United Church Board for Homeland Ministries, Philadelphia, Pa.

RACHEL HENDERLITE (*chapter 21*) is professor of religious education, Austin Presbyterian Theological Seminary, Austin, Texas.

JOHN M. LARSEN (*chapter 13*) is minister of First Congregational United Church of Christ, Everett, Wash.

J. THOMAS LEAMON (*chapter 16*) is minister of First United Church of Christ, Williamstown, Mass.

CHARLES C. LEMERT (*chapter 14*) is assistant professor of sociology/religious studies at Southern Illinois University, Carbondale, Ill.

SARA LITTLE (*chapter 2*) is professor at the Presbyterian School of Religious Education in Richmond, Va.

JAMES E. LODER (*chapter 8*) is associate professor of Christian education, Princeton Theological Seminary, Princeton, N.J.

ROBERT W. LYNN (*chapter 19*) is Auburn Professor of Religion and Education, Union Theological Seminary, New York City.

RANDOLPH CRUMP MILLER (*chapter 20*) is Horace Bushnell Professor of Christian Nurture at Yale Divinity School, New Haven, Conn.

C. ELLIS NELSON (*chapter 5*) is Skinner and McAlpin Professor of Practical Theology, Union Theological Seminary, New York City.

PHILIP H. PHENIX (*chapter 4*) is professor of philosophy and education, Teachers College, Columbia University, New York City.

EDWARD A. POWERS (*chapter 6*) is general secretary of the Division of Christian Education, United Church Board for Homeland Ministries, Philadelphia, Pa.

LETTY M. RUSSELL (*chapters 11, 22*) is assistant professor of religious studies at Manhattan College, Bronx, New York.

ROGER L. SHINN (*chapter 1*) is William E. Dodge, Jr., Professor of Applied Christianity at Union Theological Seminary, New York City.

SIDNEY B. SIMON (*chapter 18*) is professor of humanistic education, Center for Humanistic Education, University of Massachusetts, Amherst, Mass.

EDNA STUMPF (*chapter 17*) is assistant editor of *Colloquy*, Division of Christian Education, United Church Board for Homeland Ministries, Philadelphia, Pa.

JOHN H. WESTERHOFF III (*Prologue, chapters 7, 9, 10, 25, 26, Epilogue*) is editor of *Colloquy*, Division of Christian Education, United Church Board for Homeland Ministries, Philadelphia, Pa.

JOSEPH WILLIAMSON (*chapter 3*) is on the staff of the Cambridge (Mass.) Ministry in Higher Education.

D. CAMPBELL WYCKOFF (*chapter 24*) is professor of Christian education, Princeton Theological Seminary, Princeton, N.J.

A COLLOQUY ON CHRISTIAN EDUCATION

EDITED BY JOHN H. WESTERHOFF III

A PILGRIM PRESS BOOK
FROM
UNITED CHURCH PRESS
PHILADELPHIA

Library of Congress Cataloging in Publication Data

Westerhoff, John H
   A colloquy on Christian education.

   "A Pilgrim Press book."
   Bibliography: p.
   1. Religious education—Addresses, essays, lectures.
I. Title.
BV1525.W45   207'.1   72-4258
ISBN 0-8298-0238-X

In gratitude to
Carmeta
my secretary
Dick and Edna
Colloquy colleagues

CONTENTS

TRANSITION

BY JOHN H. WESTERHOFF III

These are difficult days for Christian educators. Increasingly in the local churches, laymen frustrated with their efforts at religious education and confused about their faith are asking painful questions about the meaning of the words Christian and education. Agreed-upon answers are hard to establish. And yet, the historical evidence is clear. Only when there has been common understanding in the church on the nature of the Christian faith and of education has Christian education been vital and potent.

Our current lack of agreement, therefore, suggests one way to describe the agonizing three-dimensional crisis faced by Christianity: a crisis in faith, a crisis in the local church, and a crisis in Christian education. Obviously these three are not unrelated. Thus, we cannot attempt to address the crisis in Christian education without addressing simultaneously the others, for if we lack clarity and commitment in faith we have nothing on which to base our educational efforts. And if we lack a vibrant community of faith we have no place in which to nurture people in that faith.

But we needn't lose heart. Acknowledging our crisis can be

the first step toward a new period in the history of religious education. It would do well for us to remember that the word crisis means both a critical time and a turning point. All significant changes in history have occurred in times of crisis. New movements, new vitality, new spirit, and new faith have always evolved out of just such times. That is the reason that in these days of disillusionment some of us are busy chasing rainbows. When most everyone seems to be complaining about the rain, is that really so ridiculous? Surely no one has yet found the pot of gold promised at the end of its arch. (We never expect to.) Nevertheless, a sense of humor and hope continually goad us to affirm that every dark rain cloud does have a silver lining. Anyway, singing in the rain while chasing rainbows is a more meaningful—and fun way—to live.

You can describe us as "realistic optimists." That means we live by an appreciative understanding of the past, a critical analysis of the present, and a hopeful view of the future. We believe it is wise and good to remember past rainbows, and to acknowledge the rain so as to prepare ourselves to spy and follow future rainbows to their ever-elusive reward. Yet to some we seem only to speak negatively about the way things are and what people are trying to do. Let me disassociate myself from that image as I try to make clear my feelings about the crisis and hope of church education.

After World War II church education enjoyed a flourishing life. There were differences of opinion among church educators, but these only added life to an expanding movement. During the later part of the 1960s the situation changed. Confidence in our educational programs began to wane. Today, as we enter the 1970s, too many find themselves confused and demoralized. We need to break out of that depression. We need to stop criticizing everything we've done or are doing. Everything being done is not a failure. New forms and models are being created. Relevant educational ministries are emerging in many congregations. Numerous dedicated persons are continuing to nurture children in church schools. Others are groping for and dreaming about new ways.

Our dreams are too limited. Our imaginations atrophied. Often our visions of the future do not transcend the present; rather, they only extend it. The future is with those who formulate images of the future which are radically at variance with what we now have and know. The question is: Have we lost the capacity to transcend the known, to dream impossible dreams? Can we gain the gift of imagining fundamentally alternative futures which are neither extensions of existing conditions nor choices among known feasible options? Of course we can! And that doesn't mean starting all over or stopping everything we are now doing. It means continuing our educational programs even as we set free our most imaginative church members to ask new questions and dream new dreams. Such dreaming may seem mad. But, for the health of the church, some of us may have to become "fools." I've been one for some time.

Over two years ago, I wrote *Values for Tomorrow's Children*. It represented a small contribution to the cause of the rainbow chasers—an alternative future for education in the church. The response to that tract has been more than gratifying. Not because everyone agreed with it—they didn't—but because it seems to have engendered hope and stimulated conversation among numerous laymen in local congregations about faith, the local church and education. That was its intention.

Academics wisely pointed out its inadequacies, professionals expectantly hoped for more, but laymen have used it best. In the process they appreciatively raised a number of probing questions. Some of them they have answered for themselves. Others still haunt them and me. But like all tracts, *Values for Tomorrow's Children* was meant to be timely, not timeless, a stimulant to new thoughts and actions in local churches, not a theoretical tome aimed at framing the future directions of all Christian education or answering all our questions about the Christian faith and the local church.

And yet, witnessing the practical results of those who caught the spirit of *Values for Tomorrow's Children* has renewed my enthusiasm about the future. That doesn't mean that I think Christian education and churches have been transformed. Many local churches remain unchanged. But in a significant number of places in rural, suburban, and urban settings throughout the country I have seen churches coming to life. With a rebirth of faith and commitment, new educational programs are emerging. They are all different. Few are startlingly new or worthy of press releases, but all have broken out of a bondage to the past and therefore anticipate an alternative future. Yes, there is reason to have hope.

For many church educators the break has been made, a new start begun. Yet there is much still to be done. And so another tract seemed called for. Its purpose: to engender more hope, to encourage those who have ventured forth into the unknown of new forms of educational ministry, and to provide a stimulant to further rethinking and planning for the future. The result is *A Colloquy on Christian Education*.

It is based on the many letters I have received and the many conversations I have had with laymen at workshops and lectures across the country. Typically, they are seeking a clearer understanding of Christian education, new models and designs for education in local congregations, and help in planning for the future. Their probing reveals that important questions remain to be addressed, questions like: What about the Bible? How do we pass on the richness of our tradition? Is it too late to begin with adults? Should we concentrate on the new generation? How can we build a community of faith in our day? What can we expect of the family? The list could go on. For me, such questions create a feeling of excitement in an age of transition for mainline Protestant church educators.

In just such times, I believe, it is important that we cease our criticisms and put our heads together. We need each other's help in dreaming about what might be and planning what we might do in an interim time. Too often we each try to go it alone. The theoretician works in his ivory tower and talks to his fellow academics. Practitioners frantically run off on their own, buying uncritically the latest enthusiasm hoping it will provide them with a panacea. Rarely do the theoretician and practitioners communicate. The results are tragic for both. *Colloquy* magazine has attempted to bridge that abyss. As such, it has been neither a professional "academic" nor a practical "how-to" magazine for lay educators. Its purpose has been to unite the rainbow chasers, wherever they might be and stimulate new thinking and new experimental programs to suit our age of transition.

A Colloquy on Christian Education takes a number of these attempts, most of which have been previously published in *Colloquy*, and organizes them into a book. In part, we begin where *Values for Tomorrow's Children* left off, by including essays I have written which, under other circumstances, might have been included in that book. One attempts to define Christian education, another suggests a theoretical model for Christian education, and the last outlines a process for planning an alternative future for Christian education.

But this volume aims to do more. It offers further insight into a number of the questions raised by *Values for Tomorrow's Children*. The first section contains a series of articles on the nature of Christian education; the second suggests a variety of practical designs for parish education. The last section offers diverse ways to think about and plan for the future of Christian education in the local churches.

Like *Values for Tomorrow's Children*, this book makes no great claims. My hope is that it will aid and encourage laymen in local congregations to explore new forms of religious education. It is meant to be a discussion-starter. No author in this volume would claim the whole. The essays that have already appeared in *Colloquy* are in part dated and incomplete. But like all collections of articles they can become an important educational resource for local congregations.

There is no one way to read this collection. Each article stands on its own and needs to be considered for its own merits. Some will be of more interest than others. None is to be seen as offering *the* answer. Each is a searching, probing attempt of a person concerned about the Christian faith, the local congregation and Christian education to make a contribution to the future.

Obviously, I owe a debt of gratitude to all those who have given me permission to reprint their essays, to the United Church Press who thought it important to publish them in this form, and to the United Church Board for Homeland Ministries who granted me the time and provided the stimulus to put this collection together. I humbly offer these essays as a resource for Christian education, in an age of transition.

SOUND
FOUNDATIONS

1
EDUCATION IS A MYSTERY

BY ROGER L. SHINN

Human life is a mystery, deeper than all our inquiry can fathom. And because life is mysterious, education is a mystery.

It is a good thing experts explore that mystery with the most advanced methods of science. They bring us almost daily reports, often controversial and unconfirmed, about the ways in which animal behavior illumines or obscures human behavior, about the sources of language in innate or acquired traits of personality, about preconscious processes of learning, about communication of infants or adults through body language. These collections of information and hypotheses are valuable. But after twenty-five years—I sometimes say a quarter of a century because that sounds rather awesome to me—as a professional educator, I am more impressed than ever with what I do not know about education.

I live in a society where institutions, designed to program education from infancy to the most advanced types of research, are more highly organized and financed than in any other society in all history. Yet I am impressed with the unplanned quality of many of the most significant educational experiences.

In my personal history, I suppose the most important of all educational experiences was fighting a war. What I learned was not primarily what my military teachers taught me. Neither they nor I planned that education. But it took hold. I do not therefore recommend that fighting a war be included in the educational program of youth. Plato and many others toyed with that idea. But one thing I learned in war is that I don't want to see war repeated forever.

The students I meet regularly are quick to tell me that nothing in my courses has anything like the educational impact of quite unplanned adventures of their own. For some of them, the experience of jail in a civil rights case or of a police beating in a student demonstration was a momentous educational experience. That does not mean that they or I advocate inclusion of police beatings and jail in the planned curriculum of education.

My point is that much education—perhaps the most significant education—cannot be programmed. There are times of shaking foundations, times of trauma, times of revelation that bring new apprehensions of life and the world. Often they are the very experiences that civilized and compassionate education tries to spare people. They remind us that education is mysterious and that educators had better be modest in their goals, because what they accomplish is likely to be small in relation to what they neither plan nor control.

INTENTIONAL EDUCATION

Nevertheless, intentional education is important. Most of us have faith, often challenged but not destroyed, that human beings are not simply helpless victims or beneficiaries of traumatic experiences beyond their control. If we have any sensitivity and gratitude, we realize that we are what we are because of an immense heritage painfully acquired and transmitted from ancestors who lived in caves and hovels long before we could live in heated and wired houses, who gave us a language and a technology and an inheritance of art and knowledge, along with a confidence that we could make our own new discoveries.

When I said that the greatest educational experiences for some people were war or jail or beatings, I told only part of the truth. What anybody learns in such experiences depends to a considerable degree upon what he brings to them. And what he brings to them is not simply his own sensitivity; it is an awareness that has been cultivated in home, community, church, and school.

While we should be modest about the pretensions of intentional education, we should not be timid or defeatist. Education is a mystery, but we have a mysterious ability to enter into and cultivate that mystery. Intentional education, though only a part of the constant process of education, is a valuable part. It may enable people to appropriate more momentous unintended educational experiences.

One of the unintended experiences of history—unintended, that is, as far as human planning is concerned—was the life and ministry of Jesus Christ. One consequence was the birth of a community of faith that exists to this day. The community tells the world that God loves his people—all people; that God's purpose is the liberation of mankind; that God is conquering suffering, sin, and death. The community says all this, not simply in a general sort of way, but in a very specific testimony that God has acted in Jesus Christ for these purposes.

The community of faith is not surprised that much of our culture thinks this announcement rather silly. The community, with its wavering faith, often feels a little silly saying it and is quite reluctant to live as though it believed its own story. But that does not astonish the community; it was told long ago that this news report was a "scandal"—a folly and a stumbling block—to most people, but to some the power and wisdom of God (1 Corinthians 1:24). So the community goes on telling the news in its bumbling but occasionally eloquent ways, and living it out in its half-hearted but occasionally thrilling ways. The community is never certain how important its educational efforts are. It does not believe—it certainly has no right to believe—that God's power is confined to its faltering efforts or that God loves and liberates only people who know about Christ. But it believes that it is good for mankind to know about Christ. It is grateful for what it knows of Christ and in gratitude recognizes a responsibility to tell and enact the story. It recognizes an educational mission.

THREE ASPECTS OF INTENTIONAL CHRISTIAN EDUCATION

If I distinguish three aspects of intentional Christian education, my purpose is not to separate them. They are inseparable. If they are not distinguished and perhaps labeled, one or another of them tends to get lost.

Since I have to put these in some kind of order, I shall move from the simplest—though none is very simple—to the most mysterious. I am not ranking them in importance or proposing that they form an educational sequence.

The first can be called intellectual. Christian education has an intellectual element. Part of its substance can be verbalized, told, written down. It is concerned with a historical person about whom we get information from historical records. In this sense, Christianity is quite different from Zen Buddhism or any religion that is derived exclusively from private mystical experiences or group interaction.

Furthermore, this Christian faith has all kinds of meanings for other human intellectual endeavors—for man's understanding of himself, his society, and his universe. And they have meanings for it. The faith can be understood in ways that are superstitious or profound, in ways that deepen or simply confuse human understanding.

In these days when anti-intellectualism is a vogue, it is easy to depreciate the intellectual aspect of Christian education.

Most churches do. But the anti-intellectualism is deceptive. Many students, who are quite turned off by anything called Christian education in their home churches, find an excitement and exhilaration in college courses in religion. There they may discover for the first time that Christianity has an intellectual substance worth relating to everything else they learn in the venture of higher education. Some of that excitement belongs in the local church.

The second aspect is activism. It means involvement in the world—in its suffering, its struggle, its transformation. Kierkegaard pointed out that Christ wants disciples, not admirers. But the church readily becomes a society of admirers. Active discipleship is not only a consequence of faith; it is part of education in faith.

This activism is in part political. That makes it controversial, and today the church experiences polarization as a threat. But the threat is also an educational opportunity.

Certainly, the scriptures assert the political meaning of faith. This is most obvious in the Old Testament, which tells repeatedly of war, economic struggle, and political conflict. The New Testament is rather different, but it has evident political meaning. The "kingdom" of God is a political metaphor; the beautiful Magnificat (Song of Mary, Luke 1:46 ff.) has revolutionary significance; and Jesus, quoting prophecy, said that he came "to set at liberty those who are oppressed (Luke 4:18)." Despite reluctance and fear in our churches, some of the most effective Christian education today goes on in the context of political action.

The third aspect is harder to name. It might be called education in the experience of depth. Students frequently call it "interiorization." The hunger for it today is strongest among youth, often among youth who have been saturated with intellectualization and activism. It includes a recovery of what used to be called religious experience, although everybody knows that religious experience may be shallow or deep.

Paul Goodman, not a churchman, points out that adolescent religious conversion was "once as common in the United States as in all other places and ages." Then our culture pretty nearly squelched it. "Now it seems to be recurring as a mass phenomenon." Our churches, especially the respectable denominations, don't know what to do with it. They distrust it—because it is in fact often unreliable, superficial, even artificial. So it finds outlets elsewhere—in a Woodstock festival, a hippie commune, the celebrations of the "counter culture" in which Theodore Roszak finds "a phantasmagoria of exotic religiosity."

Charles Reich, in *The Greening of America*, argues that a change of *consciousness* is more fundamental and effective than intellectual and political activity. The book is full of half-truths, but they are the halves of truth that Christian education frequently forgets. Christian education needs to recognize them, not for the sake of keeping up with the popular culture, but because Christian faith was initially a change of consciousness far more than an intellectual inquiry or a political activism. When Christian education works with the experience of depth, it enters into areas usually missed in the popular culture—prayer, self-knowledge that is frightening as well as exhilarating, agapeic love.

I must repeat that these three aspects of Christian education, although distinguishable, are not separable. I can imagine no travesties of Christian education more corrupting than a total concentration on intellectualization, activism, or interiorization. Yet such travesties do take place.

RECONSIDERATIONS

Ten years ago, I was writing a book about Christian education. It was published in 1962 as *The Educational Mission of Our Church*. It was bitterly attacked as too radical. It wasn't. It was accused of advocating "Christian maladjustment." It did.

In that book, I described Christian education in terms of

EDUCATION IS A MYSTERY

three paradoxes (not corresponding to the three aspects mentioned above): (1) growth and development in paradox with death and resurrection, (2) nurture in paradox with exposure, (3) freedom in paradox with responsibility.

Times have changed. When I wrote that book, I was worried about sociologist Philip Jacob's report that a multitude of studies had shown American college students to be "gloriously contented" and "dutifully responsive toward government" (*Changing Values in College*, 1957). Those are not the phrases used about youth today.

In looking back at my three paradoxes, I want to reaffirm all of them. Today, I would do so with some changes in accent, due to changing times. In some respects, a revised book would be more radical than the earlier one, because—as is news to no one—we are living in a revolutionary time. But it might contain some cautions missing in the earlier one, because one task of education is to say, not what the culture is saying, but what is not being said.

Today, more than a decade later, I would emphasize interiorization. I would emphasize self-understanding, self-criticism, and worship. I would warn against dogmatism and self-righteousness, so common among militants of the left and the right. I might—I'm not sure—add fourth and fifth paradoxes: youth in paradox with maturity, Christian cultural incarnation in paradox with critical perspective upon culture. Above all, I'm sure I would accent even more what I said about the mystery of selfhood and education.

2 ON THE END OF AN ERA

BY SARA LITTLE

Probably what is to be said in this article does not justify its somewhat dramatic title. But the expression is one which I used recently in a kind of spontaneous Brunerian "intuitive hunch" commentary on where we are in education. It seems to fit what I would like to say here—that the era of focus on the cognitive in both general education and church education is ended.

When did it begin? Historically, there have been recurring periods of focus on intellectual activity as the key to learning, intermixed with other periods built around a variety of emphases. Probably the most recent concentration on the centrality of the cognitive (the rational, reflective, thinking functions) appeared forcefully around 1960.

In 1959, there was the famous Woods Hole conference, summarized by Jerome Bruner in the *Process of Education*. The high priority placed on intellectual excellence in that conference may or may not have had direct correlation with the 1957 Sputnik. A 1961 statement by the Educational Policies Commission of the National Education Association stated unequivocally that the central purpose of education is "the development of the ability to think." Referring to 1918 and 1938 formulations of purpose, this 1961 statement calls attention to the immense scope projected earlier and cites the need for some principle by which decisions may be made. Thus the focus on the cognitive. Church educators, influenced by scholars like Jean Piaget and Jerome Bruner and freed from servile dependence on theologians (I speak somewhat facetiously), developed the movement toward viewing reflection as the distinctive, though never the exclusive, characteristic of the educational ministry of the church.

What has caused the change? Let me set up a few protective fences before I try to answer that question. When I say the change occurred in 1961, I only mean that something (or a configuration of things) happened which may eventuate in gradually changing values and endeavors of educators for the next few years. In considering the three questions which follow, I shall try to deal with some of the factors that have caused change—or, perhaps better, with some of the current activity or ferment that is resulting in a healthy pluralistic approach to education.

1. What is the relationship between the cognitive and the affective domains in learning and teaching?

If there has been any one dominant factor in the reassessment of the role of the cognitive domain in learning, it has been the fact that, as Max Birnbaum said in the November 15, 1969, *Saturday Review*, "during the 1960s, public education discovered the emotions." The affective domain—the feeling, valuing, emotional, aesthetic factors in human growth—has, he says, been assigned "a role as important as—or, perhaps, more important than—the traditional substantive content and skills."

For some people, reference to the affective domain brings to mind at once images of encounter groups, sensitivity training, and other human relations enterprises, in business as well as in educational institutions. For others, in the church as well as in general education, the reference becomes the increasing emphasis on the arts, or on the "expressive" activity which is such an important component in assimilating or internalizing learning. Both are categories important enough to bear extensive investigation. Both relate directly to the humanizing activity which is held to be appropriate to learning that is a "becoming," with a dimension of depth not always attached to intellectual growth.

For those of us who teach, the concern may well be with the affective component in cognitive learning. For example, a teacher, often unconsciously, has expectations or attitudes which determine whether the student can or cannot learn. Research by Robert Rosenthal of Harvard (cited in Postman and Weingartner, *Teaching as a Subversive Activity*) indicates that even rats perform better when experimenters are told the rats are of superior intelligence. Similarly, he found dramatic improvement among children about whom teachers had been told test results predicted such improvement. The implications are obvious. If minority groups are expected to be dull, they will be dull. The affective climate created by the teacher influences learning.

Or consider motivation. When a student has experienced the elation of discovery, he is motivated to continue in that heuristic approach to learning, which becomes intrinsically rewarding. The way he *feels* about what he learns *intellectually* becomes the clue to motivation. When a teacher does a good job of teaching in the cognitive domain, the response of students calls forth in the teacher that satisfying feeling of being appreciated which, in turn, motivates him to continue to improve his teaching.

Clearly, one of our tasks for the immediate future is to work toward a better understanding of the interrelationship between the affective and the cognitive domains.

2. What knowledge is of most worth?

This age-old question is again confronting us. What selective principles should guide the learner—or the teacher—into the most important areas of inquiry? Some critics of Jerome Bruner—cited by Postman and Weingartner—suggest that he "has done much to answer the question 'How do people come to know?,' but, curiously, he has not addressed himself to the question 'What's worth knowing?,' at least from the point of view of the learner." That criticism (with which I am not totally in agreement) leads me to suggest that the devotion of some of Bruner's followers to inquiry or discovery has inadvertently elevated the *act* of thinking beyond the *substance* of what is thought. We have already been in *that* trap earlier in this century.

But we are still dealing with the cognitive domain. How does the question about the worth of knowledge push us beyond it? By engaging us with the area of value-formation, which is at least as much a matter of acculturation as of rational inquiry. Constant bombardment with inconsistency between stated norms and experienced values may eventually lead to disillusionment, to the question of whether *any* knowledge at all is of worth. Or, as Margaret Mead put it in her *Culture and Commitment*, "In this century, with rising insistence and anguish, there is now a new note: *Can I commit my life to anything? Is there anything in human cultures as they exist today worth saving, worth committing myself to?*"

So we are beyond the cognitive, into the realm of the conative, of action, of socialization.

3. Is learning something that happens, or is it something that occurs as a result of intentional planning?

The question is posed too sharply, obviously. It is intended to call attention to the struggle that has existed for a long time between those who take a comprehensive view of education and those who assume a more limited definition. Among church educators, the comprehensive view is marked by emphasis on the quality of life as being the determinative factor in learning. Global statements of purpose are favored, with educational objectives indistinguishable from the purpose of the church. Among those of the second persuasion, there has been some comfort in the presupposition that, if cognitive activity is at the heart of learning, education could be intentionally planned. In fact, education might be said to have a distinctive function, and educators to be free of charges of imperialism, resulting from their apparent effort to control institutions and actions in order to educate.

Now the whole question is reopened. For example, John Westerhoff, editor of *Colloquy*, has said that "the end of education must be the welfare of the world community, and the liberation of all men." He sees education as serving "the purposes of social change, reform, and the true humanization of all peoples." To that end, he calls for a "dynamic transformation" of the educational process. Though he does not specify the nature of the process, it seems safe to assume that he is calling for a reformation of society itself as prerequisite to—or the means for—the possibility of "authentic human development."

From the consideration of this third question, then, we are led to conclude that teaching strategies related to the structure of knowledge and development of the ability to think may not be so central to education as we had fleetingly believed. But we are left with other questions. What is the relation of social action to learning? *Can* the educator—dare he—assume the mammoth responsibility called for by John Westerhoff? Indeed, what dimension of that responsibility should be assumed by other personnel of other disciplines? What, for example, of the political process as an agent of change? Or what kind of collegiality can we envision among churchmen for making possible an environment in which learning is, indeed, possible? What aspect of that joint enterprise can appropriately be assigned to the educator?

Reflections on "the end of an era" lead again to the question: Is there anything uniquely characteristic of education?

Probably so. I have some ideas, beginning with a distinction between my responsibilities as a committed Christian, a churchman, and my function as an educator. I intend to keep thinking (whether it is of the essence of learning or not) and anticipate more consideration of an important issue.

3
A PEDAGOGY FOR CHRISTIANS

BY JOSEPH WILLIAMSON

The headlines in the Boston newspapers announced recently that the public high schools of the city were being patrolled by firemen and police. The strict measures were a response by the mayor and the school committee to a series of student rebellions which had disrupted the established routines in those institutions. In the junior high school which my son attends, there have been as many as four evacuations of the building a day because of false fire alarms. It is evident that there is a general sense of crisis throughout the entire educational system of this community.

Meanwhile, the colleges and universities throughout the metropolitan area are in a period of relative stability. But one student commenting on that situation warned that it would be false to assume that all is well. On the contrary, he maintained, there is a massive disaffection with higher education which pervades the consciousness of large numbers including many members of the faculty. The high ratio of recent resignations among the university presidents testifies to the loss of confidence which they have in their own ability to lead.

The assumption underlying the remarks I wish to make

about learning is informed by my convictions that the established patterns and institutions of learning are in trouble. Given the evidences of disintegration all around, I am required in my vocation as a theologian to discern what the normative values of education ought to be in order that a movement toward reintegration may occur. Historically, Christian faith has always been closely linked with a commitment to learning. Jesus of Nazareth was affirmed by his contemporaries to be "a teacher come from God." On the basis of that acclamation, I would like to make the following judgments which ought to inform our perceptions about the dynamics of effective learning.

The first principle is that learning how to live is a larger and more urgent matter than learning how to know. This is not to say that knowledge is unimportant to life, but it is to say that knowledge abstracted from life is not adequate to the fundamental needs of the learner. Christian faith locates the focus of its attention in the life of a particular man, Jesus of Nazareth, who was confessed by his followers to be the one in whom the presence of God could be discerned. The truth of Christianity is the truth of his life and its implications for our lives. There is no way to abstract that truth out of his person and make it into a general formula which can be memorized.

In other words, at the very center of the Christian claim there is a built-in resistance to abstracting the life of the mind from the life of the body. To violate that primary insistence is to distort what is fundamental to the integrity of Christianity. And yet it is possible to say that most of the history of education in the context of Western civilization moves in the direction of that abstraction. The scientific method is both the achievement and the failure of that movement. Because the mind has been separated from the individual body, there has been on the one hand an increasing repression of the emotional vitalities of the person. What the learner feels of joy or anger is not allowed to inform the character of the learning that is going on. In the process, that learning has less and less to do with the person in his or her individual integrity and history. And, on the other hand, the abstracting tendency also serves to separate thought from action in the life of the individual. The mind becomes increasingly skilled in its analytic capacities, but it also becomes increasingly unrelated to the mobilization of those analyses for appropriate ethical activity. What one thinks and what one does are compartmentalized from each other. Rational complexity reduces the self to the state of being catatonic.

What is true for the separation of the individual mind from the individual body is likewise true for the separation of the social mind from the social body. Educational institutions are the places where the social mind is ostensibly to be cultivated. But when those institutions become isolated from the vitalities which are present in the larger social body, then education fails to take account of the fullness of life. The dominance of the technological mind in both secondary and university education is one indication of this problem. Likewise, these institutions are absolved from taking seriously the political activities which result from the knowledge which they produce. It does not seem to make any difference to the researchers that the knowledge which is formulated in the "mind" of M.I.T. is used by the "body" of the Pentagon to destroy human lives in Southeast Asia.

The Christian conviction concerning the incarnation of God in the person of Jesus the Christ means that no education which isolates the mind from the body in either a personal or a social way is adequate from a theological perspective. Knowledge is not to be gained for its own sake. Knowledge is important only as it serves the life of the whole person who exists within a whole community of other persons. There is no guaranteed method for achieving that goal. Because of the essential mysteriousness which is central to our humanity, we must say that ultimately learning to live cannot be pro-

A PEDAGOGY FOR CHRISTIANS

grammed. Some skills may be more adequate than others, but none of them can generate life. When learning is going on, the learners will evidence that by coming alive. That is the criterion by which our evaluations of what is happening in our attempts at education must be made.

The second principle for effective learning is that the knowledge of the learned can never be superimposed arbitrarily upon the person of the learner. In order to elaborate this claim, I appeal to the theological insight that God does not reveal himself to man by exerting his prerogatives as Lord, but in quite the opposite fashion. According to the Pauline hymn in the Philippian letter of the New Testament, God relinquishes, gives up, "empties himself" of those prerogatives and takes upon himself the life of a servant. He lives among his fellows as one who makes no claims about himself. In one of Søren Kierkegaard's most arresting passages, he tells the story of a king who seeks to love a maiden. But in order that she respond to him without being intimidated by his regal position, the king disguises himself as a peasant. Only under that disguise can he be confident that he is not eliciting her affection because of his authority but because she finds him to be winsome.

Much of the problem of learning in our educational institutions is rooted in the hierarchy of authority which is established between teachers and students. That problem is further complicated by the hierarchy which exists between teachers and teachers. They are graded and categorized by the number of advanced degrees they have received, by the status within the profession to which they have attained, by the number of years in teaching which they have accumulated. Their anxiety about their professional success is subsequently transferred into their relationship with those whom they are expected to teach. The result is that those who are defined as students are intimidated by the persons in authority. They are programmed by the educational process into passivity and mimicry. The important questions are set by the learned ones rather than by the learners. In Kierkegaard's terms, the response is created by the trappings of authority rather than by the inherent attractiveness of the person who would share his learning.

Recently, Paulo Freire has observed that the purpose of the teacher is not to provide the student with correct ideas about the world in which that student lives. Rather, the teacher must enable the student to discover for himself the truth of that reality as it impinges on his life. Learning does not take place as indoctrination. Learning takes place as the learner gains increasing confidence to make discoveries, to formulate judgments, to imagine the shape of what is good and beautiful and true. The teacher is invited to share in that learning, but he is not invited to legislate that learning either as a benevolent or a malevolent despot.

In the third place, learning which is congruent with the perspective of Christian faith must be carried out within the context of genuine community. I do not mean merely the given community established by the boundaries of a particular educational institution. I do mean that sense of corporate "we-ness" which is present when learners understand and act collectively in the midst of the learning process. The ministry and teaching of Jesus of Nazareth was shared with those disciples, those learners, who identified themselves with him. That sharing of their lives together was necessary to their becoming his disciples.

Unfortunately, most of what goes on under the guise of education in the United States is explicitly anticommunal in nature. Philip Slater, professor of sociology at Brandeis University, has shown in *The Pursuit of Loneliness* the pervading tendency within this culture toward isolated and fragmented forms of individualistic life. We appear to be driven toward loneliness rather than toward community. One of the most obvious places in our social system where this is evident is in educational institutions. The pervasive competition for grades and scholarships destroys any hope for corporateness. The "teacher's pet" of grade school becomes the "teaching fellow" of the university. We become sophisticated masters of sarcasm in the classroom as a way of destroying those with whom we learn. The gravest sin in the educational code is cheating—that is to say, giving assistance to one's fellow students.

The truth of the matter is that the most effective learning always proceeds in the context of communal relationships. The preliminary dynamics of learning are within the peer group of learners, not between the isolated teacher and the isolated student. Students may copy the words or the mannerisms of the teacher. They may play with the problems he poses. But those to whom the student relates most seriously and energetically are fellow students. Woodrow Wilson knew that the learning which went on in the halls and dining rooms of Princeton University was far more important than that which was taking place within the so-called classrooms. If it is true that genuine learning is experienced within the context of life among one's peers, then the responsibility of the teacher is to facilitate that process rather than to impede it. Learning means learning together. It affirms the corporateness of our lives rather than their loneliness.

The fourth principle for learning which is implied by the substance of Christian faith is the requirement to deal directly with the realities of death. To be a follower of Jesus of Nazareth meant that there could be no avoidance of his suffering and crucifixion. It meant a certain willingness to share with him in that experience. It meant, in Paul's phrase, to make up what is lacking in the suffering of Christ. Obviously, these are difficult words. But it is clear that education today tends to insulate one from the realities of death in our world rather than to cause the student to face and deal with the transformation of those realities.

Two years ago, the United States was called to consider its accountability for the war in Vietnam on Moratorium Day. The Massachusetts State Commissioner for Education instructed the teachers of the public schools to deal with the issue of the war in their classrooms. In the school which my oldest son attended, there was no mention of the war throughout the day. In response to that lack, I requested an appointment with his principal in order to register my disapproval of that avoidance. He attempted to justify the school's action to me on the grounds that junior high school students were too young to understand the complexities of the war. When I reminded him that the television reports brought that war into the living room of our home every day, he remained unmoved. He understood his responsibility as principal to include the silencing of any discussion that would be potentially provocative of criticism about the war or the United States government.

I left that attempt at conversation with a great sense of frustration about what the educational process does to people. Instead of causing them to face the harsh realities of injustice and death, it protects them from those realities. In effect, suburban schools gloss over life as it really is. They are a ghetto of isolation from the complexities of human existence outside. Because of this culture of artificiality, the students in those schools become demoralized and lose their capacities for outrage against the inhumanities of racism and war.

If learning is to take place with any kind of honesty, then it is necessary to immerse the learners in dying rather than to protect them from it. Instead of romanticizing the achievements of the technology which makes it possible for a few to walk on the moon, teachers must be willing to deal directly with the political and economic realities of what that means. They must be honest about who is making money and who is losing money in that enterprise. Learning which does not come to terms with death in its psychological and physical and cultural forms is not learning at all. It is deception. It is an exercise in not telling the truth. Not dealing with death means not dealing with life as well.

Finally, genuine learning does not take place unless it continues to open up the learner to the future possibilities of increased learning. Christian faith does not end with the death of Jesus of Nazareth. It moves beyond that death to his coming alive and to the future promise of his increasing power in the lives of men and women. If that faith is to speak to our understanding of what learning ought to be about, then we must always see the unfinished, yet-to-be-accomplished, character of what we do. Learning is never ended. It is always anticipatory. The horizon always lies beyond.

We tend to think in opposite ways. We are satisfied with the giving and receiving of grades, with the end of a semester or a year. We forget the aphorism of A. N. Whitehead that knowledge is like a dead fish: it cannot be kept. If knowledge is understood to be merely information, then learning may be finished when a given amount of data has been accumulated. But if knowledge is attained only in the on-going process of learning to live, then nothing is finally complete. Every answer provides another question. Every perception makes possible a wider world.

To conceive of learning in this way is to call in question most of our traditional methods of evaluating what has happened to the learner. Testing the learner cannot be avoided, but neither can it be carried out by requiring pupils to give back to teachers their special kinds of information and their favorite ideas. The norms by which the evaluating must be done are also the norms by which the learning must be shaped. Are the learners coming alive? Are they gaining confidence? Is community being created? Is death being confronted? Is the promise of future learning a lure to which the students are attracted? If these are in fact the standards by which the educational task is to be judged, then the evaluation which we do will appropriately apply as much to those who are the learned as to those who are the learners. To see learning in this way is to stay the forces of disintegration which do threaten most of what goes on in educational institutions today. It is also to see the possibilities of that reintegration which Christian faith affirms to be the will of God.

4
EDUCATION FOR FAITH

BY PHILIP H. PHENIX

Every community of faith claims to be the guardian and communicator of a tradition that truly interprets the ultimate meaning of human existence. This tradition the community seeks to make effective in the world and to perpetuate in each new generation. Hence education—the propagation of the faith—is an indispensable activity of the believing community.

But is it really possible to educate for faith? Is not faith a gift of grace, a consequence of the action of the Holy Spirit, which blows where it lists? Can it be a result of deliberate human nurture? One can teach mathematics, history, or even the appreciation of art—but faith, can one teach that? Is not faith like virtue, that some say can be caught but not taught?

Clearly, in a broad sense, faith is a consequence of education. People do not get faith by direct inspiration, apart from the influence of social institutions. Persons with strong Christian commitment gain it through Christian influences, and not otherwise, just as faithful Jews are created only within a Jewish fellowship.

On the other hand, it is equally clear that faith cannot be taught by any simple, foolproof method of instruction. To be sure, one can verbally communicate the doctrines that are officially accepted as true, and one can inculcate certain patterns of behavior that are characteristic of the believing community. In these respects education for faith does not differ substantially from any other type of rational instruction and socialization process. But a person can affirm the approved creeds and conform to the accepted codes of the faith community and yet be far from realizing in the core of his being the ultimate meanings these creeds and codes are intended to express. That is to say, he may be educated in the letter and form of the faith, but not in its spirit and substance.

The central question, then, is: How can the community educate for true and living faith and not merely for conformity to the accepted norms of belief and conduct within the nurturing fellowship? There are four conditions that I suggest are necessary. The first two stem from the intimate connection between faith and hope and between faith and love, respectively; the third and fourth derive from the links between faith and action and between faith and reason, respectively.

First, then, a living faith can be inspired only within a community that has hope. The adage that where there is life there is hope might better be reversed to read that where there is hope there is life. To be alive is to have one's imagination laid hold on by the palpable reality of future possibilities. That is why an education that no more than perpetuates a tradition from the past cannot beget a living faith. To be effective, the heritage must be received as a promise.

In the present period of acute social crisis the emphasis in religious education is on the divine judgment and on prophetic protest against the evils of organized life. But how does such moral indignation differ from that of nonbelievers? Can the spirit of denunciation alone beget faith? I think not. Faith cannot be communicated by desperate (literally, hopeless) people. It can be generated by association with persons who have a tenacious confidence in the possibilities of life, despite

EDUCATION FOR FAITH

the failures and contradictions that are evident on every hand. This is why the resurrection is the pivotal doctrine of the Christian community. It points to a hope that springs out of the ultimate tragedy of innocent suffering caused by organized human injustice. People who really do live day in and day out animated by such a hope can infuse a similar spirit in those who share the fellowship of faith with them.

Faith can be communicated only by those for whom it really is good news, not primarily obligation or threat. The content of the curriculum for faith must, then, include a clear and vivid presentation and celebration of the "beatific vision," the anticipation of the beloved community.

A second condition for the effective communication of faith is that those who teach do so as an expression of love. People teach for many reasons, often not admirable ones, such as the desire to control other people or to compensate for feelings of inadequacy. The one who is taught may learn the explicit lesson presented by the teacher, but at the same time, and more surely, he absorbs the atmosphere that is carried by the teacher's motivation in teaching. Faith, in the Christian sense, can be taught only by one for whom teaching is an act of loving, that is, of sensitive, responsible caring for the other.

Unfortunately, teaching is too often an attractive refuge for people who are not really capable of loving. On this account, the church is frequently confronted with the task of diverting from the work of Christian education some of those who are most eager to teach, and of seeking out and enlisting for the office others more gifted in the art of loving and on that very account more in demand for other services within the community. Yet no condition is more essential than love to the enterprise of communicating the faith.

In addition to the assurances of hope and the incentives of love, the successful imparting of faith requires opportunities for appropriate action on the part of the learner. This is but to affirm in the context of teaching the classic proposition that faith without works is dead. One can teach a literal faith by verbal instruction. A living faith, on the other hand, can be generated only in the act of living out in deed what the faith entails. To say this is not to claim that the faith is justified or validated by its practical results; in this regard the Christian understanding of life, which is not concerned with temporal success, transcends simple pragmatism. The point is rather a pedagogical one, namely, that faith cannot come alive in a person apart from its concretization in moments of significant decision.

Hence, the effective church school must break out of the bounds of merely verbal presentations of faith by linking the symbolic world of doctrine to the world of choice and deed. For every idea a channel must be sought to action. The meaning of every doctrine needs to be interpreted in terms of its exemplification in accomplishment. Such vivifying activity gives substance to the community's hope, constituting a foretaste of the life of the beloved community, and it provides a means of realizing through the learner's own life of service the import of the love extended to him by the teacher.

Finally, education for faith must take account of the life of reason. Note that I do not say "must be based on reason," for I consider it untrue that rational processes are a sure and sufficient ground for faith. A defense of faith by means of logical and scientific argument is as unpromising as its opposite, namely, the attempt to inculcate a faith that contradicts the best tested conclusions of reason and science.

How, then, does the Christian educator take account of the life of reason? As I see it, the answer lies in recognizing that reason has its source in life, that is, in a venture of faith. That is what is meant by speaking of the "life" of reason. Detached, disembodied rationality is dead.

From this standpoint, the activities of reasoning may be seen as one of the most important arenas for the exercise of faith. The opportunity of the Christian educator is to help the student see how the processes of intellectual creation and criticism exemplify the commitments of faith. For example, the learner can see the scientific enterprise—perhaps the most impressive achievement of the human spirit in modern times —as the expression of certain profound commitments to truth, to honesty in reporting, to collegial loyalty, and to social responsibility. Similarly, other intellectual endeavors, in humanistic and in technical and professional fields, can be interpreted as ways of implementing particular basic values and life-orientations, which can in turn be examined in the light of their coherence with, or divergence from, the Christian view of life.

In sum, I conclude that it is possible to educate for faith— but only under certain conditions, of which I have suggested four. Those who teach must be animated by a lively hope and motivated by love. They must provide occasions for putting faith into action in the service of others. Finally, they must relate faith to the claims of reason by showing how the life of reason is itself the expression of certain faith commitments. Even under these conditions, there is no guarantee that the light of faith will shine brightly in those who are taught. But some such concept of education seems to me to provide for the creative action of the Holy Spirit.

5
TEN RIGHTEOUS PEOPLE

BY C. ELLIS NELSON

RELIGION IS ONE OF THE
MOST COMPLICATED HUMAN CONCERNS

Worship today ranges all the way from silent prayer to boisterous celebrations with guitars and firecrackers. Academic theology ranges all the way from "the threat of nothingness" through formal church theology to exalted views of the whole cosmos pulsating with God-energy. Ethical issues as seen by many young people are what society does with and for the poor, the lonely, the dispossessed, the powerless—while many adults see these same human conditions as the judgment of God on people who don't have the will to work.

How do we make sense out of all this?

Our usual way is to go to the Bible to get our bearings and then "apply" our findings to the present. But this doesn't get us very far. We usually find in the Bible the presuppositions we already have. Hawks can find justification in the Bible for American participation in the Vietnamese civil war. Doves can probably show that the Bible advises that we get out as soon as possible.

Another way to make sense out of contemporary religion is

to listen to the church. This may seem hopeless because there are so many points of view in the church about everything. Yet the church with all its faults has ambled along through a lot of history; and, when it does "take on" an issue such as social justice for blacks and other oppressed people or economic systems that allow harsh poverty, it can in a few years develop a position which represents the enlightened Christian attitude toward these matters. This comes about because the church is a community of people who have to some degree subordinated their ideas and energies to a search for what God wants for human life today. The Bible is naturally a part of such a process. But the Bible needs prayerful and corporate study over a period of time by the church to produce beliefs that can properly be accredited to the Holy Spirit.

The church is not infallible. It has made monstrous mistakes in the past, such as fighting wars instead of being a reconciling agent, supporting slave trade in America rather than liberating black human beings, and turning the free forgiveness of God into a commodity that can be bought with cash. Knowing this weakness, Protestants have in their theological bloodstream the conviction that no person and no institution can take away the right and responsibility of every individual to stand before God and to account to God for his life.

So the Protestant Christian is in an almost impossible psychological and religious situation. He must participate in the life of the church (or some community of believers in Christ) or he can't be a Christian in the biblical sense; yet he has to rely on himself and stand up for his own beliefs or he can't be true to his only authority—God. The Protestant somehow has to live out his life in tension between these two sources of power.

But do we want to think of our Christian faith as being caught between two powers that stand against each other? How can we gain increasing satisfaction from our faith rather than be constantly wondering whether our religious ideas and impulses are right and therefore should be vigorously pushed, or whether they are misconceptions that should be overruled by friends in the church? There is and can be no solution to this problem, given our Protestant belief that the individual is responsible to God. However, there is another way we can think and act about the problem.

FAITH AND PERSONALITY

Gordon Allport was, until his death a few years ago, a professor of psychology at Harvard University. He gave a lot of attention to problems of prejudice in religion. There are many studies done by social scientists showing that church people are as prejudiced as (or more prejudiced than) nonchurch persons. Since Judaism and Christianity both exalt love of neighbor, it is strange that the reverse attitude seems to be operative. Allport, puzzled over this situation, developed the idea that religion must be considered a part of a person's psychological make-up and then suggested that, broadly speaking, there are two types of religious persons.

One type he labels the extrinsic type. This person uses religion for deep psychological needs. He tends to deal with the externals of religion, such as committees that manage the institutional aspect of the church. He uses the church fellowship for his loneliness, he hears only the preaching which supports his views, he makes social contacts with families that support his way of life, or he enjoys the music and worship because it relieves his tensions.

The intrinsic type Allport sees as a person who is seriously searching for meaning in his life as something that is important to him, regardless of what others think. He attempts to pull together all the experiences he is having and sees them in relation to his idea of God so that his life has a constant alertness to new meaning. Such a religious outlook means that the person is able to transcend somewhat his own self-centeredness and attempts to be an agent for better human relations.

Allport worked out tests for the extrinsic and intrinsic religious types and then tested their degree of prejudice. Needless to say, the intrinsic type of religious person is a tolerant person, while the extrinsic type is a person who prejudges others and who uses religion to support his psychological need. Obviously, this division of people into two types is crude, but it is a useful way of thinking about the motives that support the religious life.

THE FAITH QUESTION

If we use Allport's way of thinking about religion, we can play down the old question of where the authority is in religion—whether it is in the person, the Bible, or the church. We are free to turn our attention to the question of how real (intrinsic) religious faith is developed. This does not make our problem easier, but it does focus our minds on the central issue: How can we foster faith? Faith itself is a gift of God (Ephesians 2:8), but striving for faith is our task (Philippians 2:12).

The major thing we must keep in mind is that faith resides in, and arises out of, a community of believers; therefore, anything we can do to build a mutual respect and a desire to care for and about other persons is a fundamental element of faith. Translated into practical terms, this means that we may have to limit the size of congregations in order to create a human environment in which individuals can experience spiritual values. At once you see the problem: American churches often use business as the model, where larger size can be more efficient. But efficient for what? The church should be processing human attitudes, trying to imagine a better future and how to build it, helping people to forgive each others' sins, steadying persons going through circumstances that might drive them to drink or drugs, celebrating the goodness of earth and life's happy events. These things require fairly intimate fellowship and much conversation. They cannot be manufactured on schedule by a machine.

Do we have nerve enough to limit the size of a congregation according to its role in fostering faith? If we do, then our next step is to see the congregation as a group of people—all sorts, conditions, and ages—who are striving for an understanding of faith in the light of the experiences they are having. Translated into practical terms, this means that classifying children by age and putting them in cubicles for one hour a week with a woman teacher may begin to look like a striving for efficiency rather than faith. If church people ask the faith question, they might get faith answers. They might see that a married couple who took children of various ages on short trips on Saturday and then took them home for food, fun, prayer, and serious probing of the Bible and their experiences made more sense and needed no buildings! Grouping of families for similar purposes might achieve the same end.

Once a person puts on the spectacles that look for the way faith can be fostered or enhanced, a lot of conventional church practices appear odd. Why is it that women meet separately and study the mission of the church? Why are there men's Bible classes? Why do church people claim to be sinners and pray every Sunday for forgiveness and yet will seldom allow other sinners to pray with them in public? People who feel that they have failed and have taken a drink are usually not welcome in church. People who have failed in their marriage and other matters often drift away. Why?

Why do adolescents drift away from church and seldom return until they have married? We will never answer that question by saying we need more communicants' classes or better parties. What adolescents need and want is human companionship through which they can be helped in their desire to come of age; that is, persons with responsibilities and respect. Such an adolescent need is human and requires understanding human responses in the nonrational way a baby needs affection.

If we ask the faith question, we will not see the congregation as being limited to a gathering of people on Sunday for public worship but as a group of people with a common commitment to Christ and a desire to understand their faith. The faith view changes the nature of the business and institutional problems of the congregation. Buildings will be viewed in terms of their use by the congregation and community. Employment practices will be seen in terms of justice and not in terms of the lowest possible salary scale the church can offer. Such matters become curriculum for study groups, whether these be short-term committees or regularly scheduled classes, because what is done with these problems shows the faith by which the congregation is living. Suburban or white middle-class churches need to brood about their life style and how their decisions affect the social and political order which increasingly packs black and brown people into the central part of the city which in turn makes for a life style that corrupts people, police, and politicians. Once the "eye" becomes adjusted to the spectacles of faith, a person tends to be less self-centered and more human-centered as Allport pointed out—less interested in fixing blame and more concerned about the basic rights of other people.

You take it from here. My mind is too stimulated. What would happen, for example, if your denomination did not send printed curriculum to the congregation for a year but instead said, "Use your lives, your congregational problems, and your community situation as the substance for discussion." Faith, of course, is always home grown. Perhaps we are afraid of faith, and that is why we feel safer if we import our discussion topics from Philadelphia!

You will recall from Genesis, chapter 18, that God was ready to destroy Sodom because of its wickedness, but Abraham pleaded that the righteous people there should not be punished with the wicked. After the bargaining ended, God said, "For the sake of ten [righteous people] I will not destroy it."

Such is the power of a few who see with the eyes of faith.

6
ON KEEPING ONE'S BALANCE

BY EDWARD A. POWERS

THE ROLE OF TRADITION IN EDUCATION

Tevye, the play's leading character, describes life as like a *Fiddler on the Roof*.[1] "And how do we keep our balance?" Tevye asks rhetorically. "That I can tell you in a word," he answers his own query. "Tradition!"

Tevye in "Fiddler" goes on to explain the function of tradition: "Because of our traditions, everyone knows who he is and what God expects him to do." Tevye has described in a vital way the function of religious tradition in conferring identity and a framework for thought.

The role of tradition has been strong in Judaism and in Roman Catholicism. For Catholics, the magisterium or teachings have been central, binding upon pope and parishioner alike. For Protestants, tradition has until recently been a stumbling block. Luther's revolt against the Catholicism of his day set scripture over against tradition. "Sola Scriptura" became a battle cry in the religious wars of Europe in post-Reformation days.

A major result of the ecumenism of the mid-twentieth century has been a new understanding of scripture and tradition on the part of both Catholicism and Protestantism. Protestants have come to see the role of tradition in their life and thought. The tradition has taken its rightful place with scripture as one of the twin resources for the life of the community of faith.

IN SEARCH OF MEANING

Webster gives three meanings of the word which have a bearing on the purpose of this article. The word itself comes from the Latin *traditio* meaning "an action of handing over." Thus, tradition has an active, sequential dimension. The word "traditioning" has been coined to describe the process of handing on the tradition.

A second meaning is "a belief or practice or the totality of beliefs and practices not derived directly from the Bible but arising and handed down within the Christian community originally by oral tradition." Sometimes the word is used to define the individual belief or practice. At other times the word tradition conveys the whole of belief and practice.

A third definition is "a line of historical continuity or development marked by distinctive characteristics." This definition would apply to diverse human experience—the arts, science, literature, sports.

The definition, then, has several component parts: continuity with the past, a clear shape, both belief and practice, an active sense of conveyance from one to another.

People often say, "We should teach the heritage, the tradition!" The comment is frequently made with considerable intensity of feeling. This chapter will try to suggest why and how such teaching can take place.

WHY FOCUS ON THE PAST?

It is no longer self-evident that history is functional and that the past is an infallible storehouse of wisdom. Much of the youth revolt against tradition and history comes in the face of the radical changes of the present which seem to render obsolete much of conventional wisdom or historical precedent. The question, then, is: Why focus on the past? The Hebrew-Christian *view of God* is in part rooted in past event. God is spoken of as Creator, Judge, and Redeemer and the evidence is to be found in past event. God has acted in past events and we know who he is by the ways he has revealed himself. Sometimes Christianity is spoken of in terms of the "scandal of particularity," the surprising ways God is to be known in specific events. God has revealed himself in particular events: the Exodus, the Babylonian captivity, the coming of Jesus, the crucifixion and resurrection, Pentecost.

A second answer to the "why" question comes from the *Hebrew-Christian view of history.* History is regarded as "history," the arena in which God acts and in which his people live out their covenant. E. Harris Harbison speaks of Christianity as a "history-valuing tradition." [2]

Hans Meyerhoff goes perhaps even further in relating the Hebrew-Christian tradition to historical consciousness:

Israel and Christianity . . . did not awaken the ancient world from its unhistorical slumber. What they did was (a) to charge history with a religious significance which it had not had previously and (b) to read the progression of history as a clue to the design and direction imposed upon it by God's will. The historical world assumed a new significance because certain events in it such as Israel's covenant with God or the temporal existence of Jesus, were imbued with a crucial symbolic meaning. Moreover, these events and others were interpreted as part of an over-all pattern of history which exhibited a meaningful movement and direction from its obscure origins in the Book of Genesis to a redemptive, eschatological goal in or beyond history. In both these respects, the Jewish or Christian tradition expressed a new type of historical consciousness, which has become the characteristic conception of history in the Western World.[3]

The primary answer to the question of "why" relates to our *identity*. We are the creatures even if not the captives of our history. Our identity is formed out of the forces of our past and of our people's past. James Baldwin in a vital passage on "The White Man's Guilt" speaks in somewhat universal terms about history and personal identity. "History is not merely something to be read. . . . The great force of history comes from the fact that we carry it within us. . . . It is to history that we owe our frames of reference, our identities, and our aspirations."[4]

As Christians, we are part of a people who have experienced God and life in particular ways. We have developed beliefs and practices which are dependent upon that experience and the experience of our ancestors in the faith. No adequate understanding of the liturgy can be developed without the sense of historical perspective and continuity. The church gathers around a table through which events of the original Last Supper are re-enacted. That act has a kinship with every breaking of bread with kin and friend.

Christians come to their past not as those fascinated with historical oddities but as those whose life is shaped in significant part by that heritage. Abraham, Isaac, and Jacob are not only interesting people. They are our ancestors in the faith whose way of walking has helped direct our paths.

This approach has great consequences for Bible teaching. From this perspective, events of the Bible such as the exodus and the resurrection are not alone acts of deliverance of an ancient people. They are a part of our story, paradigms of our future. The God who led Israel out of Egypt leads his people out of present lands of bondage.

FOCUS ON THE PRESENT

As is obvious from speaking of tradition in relation to identity, the focus is not upon the past but on the present. Gordon Kaufman has this in mind in writing of the Christian's dependence upon tradition and the events which have given it birth:

His work is rooted in the conviction that it is through an understanding of those events that the real meaning of human existence is grasped. Hence, the concern of theology to relate those decisive events to contemporary existence arises not out of slavish subservience to external authority but out of the sincere and responsible pursuit of truth itself.[5]

Tradition provides for us two resources: *guidelines* and *faith*. Jesus in the Sermon on the Mount (especially Matthew 5:17–48) demonstrates the living quality of these *guidelines*. He described his mission not as the abolishing of "the law and the prophets" but their fulfillment. According to Jesus, the commandment, "You shall not kill," is to be seen not alone as the actual destruction of another's life but anger, insult, and labeling others ("You fool!") are also forms of person-killing. Thus, hatred, racism, sexism, enmity, stereotyping are evil because they violate the guideline of person-affirmation.

Another guideline is suggested in Genesis 1: God has created the world and called all of it good. Thus, that which affirms and fulfills the created order is good. That which destroys the created order—pollution, war, wearing out of the soil without replenishment—is evil and God denying.

The guidelines are not always self-evident. Nor are they fixed in cement. Jesus, knowing the tradition, could give it life in applying it to a new situation. Thus, he associated adultery with lust, murder with hatred.

An excellent illustration of the approach to guidelines, the living tradition, is found in a Jewish group in Pennsylvania which has started a "Trees for Vietnam" project. The interpretive material on the project says:

It is written in the Torah: "When you shall besiege a city a long time, in making war against it to take it, you shall not destroy the trees thereof by wielding an axe against them; for you may eat of them, but you shall not cut them down." Jewish tradition has always recognized the need to support life and all that sustains life. Out of this tradition has come a call to aid in the reforestation of a defoliated, war-torn country.

The tradition also gives us *resources for faith.* The Christian community is a covenant community in part because our ancestors in the faith are men and women of the covenant.

Tradition cannot give faith but it can point to faith. The educator can share with students the signposts of faith which map terrain similar to that which we face today. The models of resistance to tyranny and injustice seen today in the Berrigans were first acted out by the prophets, John Hus, Martin Luther, Joan of Arc, and Dietrich Bonhoeffer.

The tradition provides a social vision—utopian or otherwise. Take as an example the notion of Shalom which occurs with remarkable frequency in the Old Testament. The word is a synonym for the English words well-being, wholeness, justice, peace, and community. The vision of the peaceable kingdom in which the whole created order is in harmony is the Bible's utopia.

God, the Bible demonstrates, seeks shalom for his people. Shalom is not some futuristic, idealized utopia. It is God's gift now. In the absence of its full realization, a concept such as shalom can provide an energizing vision for Christian teaching, learning, living.

THE THRUST IS FORWARD

The power of tradition as identity-forming must be coupled

with the Christian doctrine of hope because the *thrust* of tradition is forward.

Tradition for Christian or Jew is different than fate for the Greek. We are not locked into some historical determinism in which the past guards the future's gate. As James Baldwin was suggesting, the past may give us our frames of reference but it doesn't necessarily proscribe the future. The Christian believes the springboard for the future is to be found in the tradition. What is past is indeed prologue.

Tradition gives us signposts of the future. Jesus had this in mind, when in Matthew 16 he talked about signs and the weather: "When it is evening, you say, 'It will be fair weather; for the sky is red.' " He chides his listeners, "You know how to interpret the appearance of the sky, but you cannot interpret the signs of the times." Jesus is pointing to the calling to read the signs in the light of the gospel and the tradition.

When one thinks of history in terms of teaching, he finds he must deal with the notion of *events*. An event is not simply an occurrence or happening but one which has special significance. A paradigmatic event may be thought of as one which offers a paradigm or model of significant experience which has a wider meaning. Thus, the Easter event is not just a historical occurrence or even the belief of a particular people about how God has acted in their past. It also contains the seeds of hope—the God who raised Jesus has triumphed over death and sin. Indeed, even as Exodus is the dramatic announcement that God is for the liberation of his people, Easter is the paradigm of new life and hope in the face of overwhelming defeat.

From tradition's storehouse, the Christian teacher or learner does not draw simply archaic junk. What he draws are the guidelines for future life and work based upon the meaningfulness of past event.

TEACHING TRADITION

The tradition was born in the life of a people. The faith in God as deliverer, lawgiver, hope, and love was not kindled through idle speculation. That faith was born within a people's common life in the face of enemies, plague, bondage and exile.

The faith community is itself a major resource for Christian teaching. The young learn about the tradition through the ways it functions today in the life of the community of faith—through liturgy, life style, frames of reference. Much of this is implicit and the product of the environment of the church's life. Much of the tradition, too, is oral. The young child learns about Jesus' birth or Easter or Thanksgiving from parents or the media. On the other hand, he experiences the meaning of these events in a communal context.

The liturgy depends strongly on scripture and tradition. As the congregation celebrates its life corporately, it re-enacts or re-presents the great events and meanings of its heritage. The church year itself has this dramatic quality. Thus, Christian teaching should focus in significant part upon liturgical experience and material. Persons learn a great deal both by imitation and by reflection upon experience. Both modes have important links with liturgy.

If it is true that the thrust of tradition is future-oriented, a demanding task is placed upon church educators—reconceiving the tradition in new situations. If it took God an incarnation to embody his message, we will not do with less. The guidelines of person affirmation, fulfillment of the created order, and shalom must be concretized in actual situations where clear alternatives exist.

The tradition has no validity in its own right. It is a storehouse of memory and a resource for hoping. Any vitality it has is in the God whose remembered acts it conveys and whose promise for justice and peace it carries. Thus, the issue is not teaching the tradition but, rather, learning from humanity's past experience with God what the shape of hope appropriately is.

Thus, the tradition becomes a treasury out of which to understand life anew. But understanding comes fully only with a heavy dose of faith. The God whom our fathers knew will be the God of our children. But that is finally an act of faith—in God and in our children.

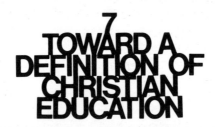

TOWARD A DEFINITION OF CHRISTIAN EDUCATION

BY JOHN H. WESTERHOFF III

Defining Christian education is no easy endeavor. Take either of these words separately and the task is difficult; put them together and it becomes immense. Of course, not everyone has this difficulty. Some people have little trouble with an answer. Typically they respond:

> A Christian is a person who believes that Jesus is his Lord and Savior, belongs to and worships in a Christian church, reads the Bible and tries to act according to its teachings. Education is what goes on in Sunday school where people learn about Jesus and the Bible.

Such a simple explanation has never satisfied me. I continue to search for a more meaningful understanding.

Exploring the early Hebrew understanding of education, I found that they believed education to be the means whereby we aid persons to grow into a likeness of God. (That was distinctly different than the classical view which tended to see education as primarily an intellectual enterprise.) They understood it as primarily moral, that is the formation of the good man—the one who knows and does what is right. Convinced that persons need to learn to be good and that the sacred scriptures contained the key to right living, they affirmed the need to engage in a long and arduous study of "The Torah." Through such activity, a person came to know how to live correctly, and thereby acquire salvation.

Christianity perpetuated a like conviction, namely that the purpose of education was to insure proper morality and salvation (i.e., wholeness, health and oneness with oneself, one's neighbors and God). Following that lead, the Protestant Reformation, even as it professed the conviction that salvation was through faith alone, stressed that faith was best approached through careful study of its source—the Bible. As a result, education in Protestant churches was primarily aimed at the study of God's word and the formation of good character.

It would be difficult to make a case against salvation as one central aim of Christian education. However, that word needs some unpacking. For me, salvation means to be set free to wander in the world as a pilgrim. This is the image of salvation I find permeating every page of the Bible. In the exodus where the people are delivered out of bondage and set loose to wander to a place they do not know, salvation and freedom are closely related. And the image of the free person is the pilgrim, the one who has no worldly home and yet is at home in the world, the one whose hope does not reside in his own efforts and yet believes his efforts can serve his God, who acts in the world through men. The result of such freedom is the ability to venture in the world as a stranger and alien with a vision of a new world. In this way, salvation is closely tied up with faith, with the way we look at the world and understand our place in it. Understanding faith as a world view and value system led me to think of Christian education in anthropological terms. The anthropologist speaks of education as the transmission of cultural heritage. All people have a culture. Their culture consists of the shared products of human learning. This learned behavior includes such tangibles as tools, shelter, and clothing; and such intangibles as language, aspirations, values, attitudes, and beliefs. Education is the process by which men pass on that culture.

Religion is one central aspect of every culture. At least we have no record of any culture which has survived that hasn't had religion. Every piece of evidence points to the assumption that one of man's basic needs is to make sense of the universe, the natural world, and his relationship within it. Though not shared with other creatures, this need is as deep as hunger and thirst.

Man's expression of religion is important for it provides him with a way of looking at the world and understanding his place in it. As an aspect of his culture it is learned. The process by which it is learned begins with a person's earliest experiences and is essentially unconscious. It was this understanding of education which influenced my thoughts in *Values for Tomorrow's Children.*

My argument in that book pressed the point that educators needed to make the total life of the community of faith and all the experiences a person has with or within it the focus of our educational concern. My message was simply this: If our concern is with Christian education we cannot restrict our attention to church schools for education is not synonymous with schooling. It was to give proper weight to all the other educating forces in the church and to enlarge the focus of church educators to include the total life of the community of faith that I addressed my concerns. In contrast to some educational theorists who distinguish between education and schooling by linking the concept of education to enable students to think straight and apply what they learn to life, I make education broader than schooling, approaching what some have called nurture.

Some of my critics believed that I claimed too much for education. They pointed out that if education is concerned with everything that goes on in the life of the church and the lives of its members, then it is concerned with nothing. There is some truth in that position. Surely education is a specific concern in the church's total ministry. Yet I insist that education as a specific concern in the church's total ministry must still focus on every aspect of the church's life! However, I remain aware that such a claim does not solve our problem of definition. We still need clarity on what we mean by Christian education, if for no other reason than it is impossible to evaluate or plan our educational ministry without such understanding.

And so, aware of the complexity of the problem, I hazard a definition. It is a working definition, a basis for discussion. I state it this way: *Christian education is those deliberate, systematic and sustained efforts of the community of faith which enable persons and groups to evolve Christian life styles.* Education defined in this way clearly is concerned with how persons look at the world and understand their place in it. It implies a broad understanding of the educational process but more limited than what the anthropologist terms enculturation, for it implies conscious purposefulness.

But so far we still only have a series of words called a definition. We need to explore what those words mean. To do so, we have divided our definition into three parts. Christian education is:

1. Deliberate, systematic and sustained efforts of the community of faith. These first three words provide a key to my understanding of education. Obviously learning is happening all the time, but education as defined is different. For learning to be education it needs to be deliberate, that is, planned, purposeful, and intentional. Education assumes efforts that we consciously set out with reason to engage in. Learning to be education also needs to be systematic. That is, it needs to be seen as one effort or set of efforts within the context of numerous other efforts all aimed in some coherent direction. And last, learning to be education needs to be sustained. Single isolated efforts have minimal effect. Education assumes a significant number of connected efforts over a long period of time. Thus, Christian education implies a sustained, holistic series of intentional effects.

In other words, according to my definition, education is something particular. That doesn't mean I have discarded my concern for all the many ways in which persons learn. For example, we should never forget that a person can tell a group of black and white children that they are all loved equally, but if that person puts her arms around a white child and unconsciously holds back contact with a black child, a different message is communicated, a different lesson is learned.

Studies on prejudice and sexism in Protestant church school curriculum revealed that when the curriculum was consciously dealing with the relationships between people and male/female roles, it came off pretty well; but throughout the rest of the curriculum prejudice and sexism were discovered. The expressed and hidden curriculum differed—the hidden was more powerful. And thus, in the long run, what was actually learned was the opposite of what we intended to teach.

So much of our most significant learning is unconscious. For example, a church whose customs for years have dictated silence in the church prior to its service of worship, the avoidance of personal contact with others in the pews or the sharing of emotion during the service will have difficulty getting its members to engage in a contemporary community celebration. We learn all the time. My conviction is that this hidden curriculum, this unconscious learning, is so important we cannot afford to let it remain unconscious. We need to look at the total learning experience of people and bring as many aspects of it into our conscious, deliberate, systematic, and sustained efforts. That is what it means to make learning education.

This implies that when we set out to communicate our biblical tradition we become conscious of the context in which we communicate, the methods we use, and the related experiences one has in the community which claims that tradition, for in the final analysis all of these will influence what is truly learned.

What might that mean? Well, one central and widespread view in the scriptures is the unity of word and deed. The creation story in Genesis provides the paradigm: God said, "Let there be light" and there was. Here there is no separation between word and deed. Then there is the famous passage from Isaiah, where Isaiah exclaims that the word of God shall not go forth and return without being fulfilled. People asked Jesus who he was. His answer: Look around and see what is happening—the captives are freed, the sick cured . . . In fact in the Gospels it is this pointing to deeds which is central to the claim that Jesus *is* the Word. Continuously the Word of God is identified in the scriptures by acts.

The Bible makes no separation between mind and body, thinking and doing. They are one. The emphasis is always on what we are—that is, the union of what we know and what we do.

It seems obvious to me that one will have difficulty acquiring this perspective on life unless one's experience within the community of faith is one in which at every moment of time, thinking and doing are unified. This is what my friends mean by an action/reflection model for Christian education. The attempt to translate that theory into practice is an attempt to take our biblical tradition very seriously, while at the same time it implies the need to expand the church's educational ministry to include its total life.

The first part of my definition then aims at making as much learning as possible in the church into education: that is, to make the hidden dimension of significant learning in the church visible, deliberate, systematic and sustained.

2. Efforts which enable persons and groups to evolve. The educational process is at best a facilitating process. It is not so much something the educator does or makes happen but rather something the educator encourages or aids. Learning is finally something which happens in the personal life of the learner. At best the educator can set up conditions and aid in that process. Education is a humble task which affirms the consciousness and personhood of each learner, but also assumes responsibility for learning.

To describe enabling or facilitating is to speak about those particular qualities which exemplify those who help others to learn. One essential quality is that he is a learner himself who joins with the learner in a shared experience or action. Another quality is an attitude which understands and prizes the learner—his feelings, opinions, and his personhood.

Such a person participates in a process which begins with the learner—his needs, his problems, his questions. He provides a multitude of diverse resources which offer to the learner experiences relevant to his needs.

To act in a facilitating or enabling process for education is to affirm certain assumptions. They go like this: Human beings have a natural potentiality and desire for learning. Significant learning takes place when what is to be learned is perceived by the learner as having relevance for his own purposes, and the most significant learning is acquired through action when the learner participates in the learning process.

The role of the facilitator is to set the climate and mood for the learning experience, to aid the learner in his own significant learning, to be a flexible resource for the learner. In my definition, this educational process of facilitation is addressed to both persons and groups.

Suggesting that education is aimed at persons needs no comment, but we would like to emphasize the need to expand our educational concerns to groups. We cannot afford any longer to fasten too obsessively or exclusively on "the person." Pascal once said, "One Christian is no Christian." It is doubtful if we can speak of the "healthy individual" unless we also talk about the healthy family, community, group. Groups like individuals have a personality and life. They are more than the conglomerate of individuals: The story of man is the story of groups. Man is not a solitary animal. He has always lived in groups. He fulfills his humanity in community. Increasingly we are beginning to understand that you cannot fully influence a person and forget his family, his peer groups, his associates, and the others with whom he comes in contact.

To be concerned for groups is to take seriously where and how persons learn. I can remember when we used to take a minister out of his church and to a retreat center with other ministers for an educational experience. We then sent him back to his church. The result was an unchanged or frustrated minister. In fact, the more he learned in this way the more dysfunctional he often became in his church. It should have dawned on us sooner that we were forgetting the groups in which he lived and worked. It is now more common to invite a minister and a number of his lay leaders to such educational programs. By working with them as a supportive community, a group, they are able to learn in ways that make them more functional when they return to their local church.

Not only do persons learn better in groups, group learning itself is more important for Christian education than personal learning. Simply put, education which is not social is not Christian.

Lastly, the word evolve in my definition points to the realization that Christian education is a lifelong process. It begins at birth, perhaps at conception, and extends to death. For too long we have begun to plan for education when a child goes to the first grade (before that it's called babysitting) and extend our educational program until graduation from high school (if we can keep them that long). We seem to forget that some of the most significant learning in a person's life might be the years from birth to six. We also seem to forget that developmentally certain kinds of learning, for example, high levels of moral thinking, may be impossible to learn until the post-high school years. Without wanting to discount the middle-childhood years, I'd like to make sure that the educator plans Christian education from birth to death. What might that mean in the coming years?

An anthropologist friend of mine was concerned with how most people in our culture use and misuse their environment. She discovered that people in other cultures behaved differently. She felt that perhaps the earliest experience a child has influences the way he looks at the world and behaves toward his environment. She discovered that in our culture most often the baby is born in a hospital, the doctor takes the baby from the mother, uses suction to draw mucous from the baby's throat and only returns the baby to the mother many hours later. Could that experience be a key to why we act as we do?, she asked. Perhaps. In many other cultures the baby is born, crawls up the mother and immediately begins nursing, reversing the mucous through his system. The baby has immediate contact with his mother, feels at one with his world, and so forth. She decided to convince the doctor to let her have her baby in this manner because she was concerned for the way her child would feel about the world. My point is that concern for such questions needs to be part of religious education.

3. Christian life styles. The purpose of this lifelong educational process is the development of what can be discerned as Christian life styles in persons and groups. To simply promote settings for learning is meaningless. It is a particular kind of learning, aimed at political ends that is the concern of educators. All of life is a vehicle for learning, but not all learning is education. To be education learning must have some clear goal that is agreed upon by the community who is engaged in education.

Christian describes "the content" and "the process." Both the means and end of the Christian education enterprise need to be Christian. It would take more than a few paragraphs to unpack that word. The best way I know to talk about Christian is to say it describes a particular way of looking at the world—a particular understanding of ultimate reality, the world, man and his life in community. To summarize that understanding would be impossible. But let me try another way of thinking about the means and end of Christian education in the light of the meaning of the word Christian.

If we were to take the usual major divisions of concern used in Christian education we would have Bible, Church History, World Religions, Theology, and Ethics. To characterize the questions which have dominated each of these concerns we could say the Bible question has been: What does the Bible say? The church history question: What happened in the history of the church? The world religions question: What do other men believe? The theology question: What do we believe? And the ethics question: What is right and wrong? All of these are what questions, information-content questions which can be addressed in classrooms with textbooks and instructors. After one has learned the answers and wishes to claim them, he can say I am a Christian.

But such questions may not be the right questions for Christian educators to address. Let me suggest another set of questions which I think shed more light on the word Christian. In this case the Bible question is: How did the people of God learn to see God acting in history? The church history question: How did the community of faith respond to God's acting in history in the past? The world religions question: How has God revealed himself to other men? The theology question: How do we discern where God is acting in history today? And the ethics question: How do we act so as to join him in his history making?

Such questions are process questions. They are difficult to

answer in a classroom with a textbook and instructor. They are questions best answered in a group which is involved in the process of attempting to be Christian. To be able to answer and act upon these questions is to discern how Christian we are.

That brings me to the final words in my definition of Christian education—life style. For too long the primary concern of education has been thinking, intellectual function, that is, an activity of the mind aimed at knowing something or about something. We forget, or so it seems, that a person is a thinking, feeling, acting person. The words life style pick up those three aspects of human behavior and hold them together. It isn't enough that Christians think of certain things in certain ways. The Christian is called to feel and to act as a whole person. Christian education which does not take man's total behavior—life style—seriously is simply not Christian. For too long we have neglected the realm of the affections. For example, one important theme in the Bible is wonder or awe. I would argue that when people experience wonder or are in a state of awe they are very close to a biblical view of life, very close to understanding our world and ourselves through the eyes of faith. But how often do we concern ourselves with such emotions in the life of the church?

I would further maintain that thinking and feeling by themselves do not make man any better. Thinking and feeling are only important to the extent that they permit and enable men to act. Education must be understood increasingly in the way it frees men to act in the public sphere of life—within and upon our institutions—with others in the community. To be engaged in Christian education we must seek ways by which thinking, feeling and acting are successfully related. To do so is to be concerned about life styles.

There we have it. Christian education focuses on the total life of persons in the faith community and it is the deliberate, systematic and sustained efforts of that faith community which enable persons and groups to evolve Christian life styles.

8 THE MEDIUM FOR THE MESSAGE

BY JAMES E. LODER

McLuhan has made the medium more significant than the content; he has, in gestaltist terms, effectively reversed figure and ground. Before, we looked almost exclusively at content; it is now our duty to note well the message the medium creates, or, perhaps better, the fashion in which the medium creates us.

Actually, McLuhan is not at all the first to do this for the American cultural scene. One of the most significant earlier exponents of "the medium" was John Dewey. His metaphysics of experience and the stress upon process and its power to create human nature and knowledge opened the doors and windows of the dark, dull, dry American version of classical education; he let in a lot of light and fresh air but also some smog. When the medium creates the message by fashioning in some persistent but subliminal way the general frame of reference within which all one's hearing, speaking, and learning takes place, then it behooves us to take a long look at it.

It is a little too early to know about McLuhan as a "medium" spreading media prophecies, but we can look at some of the factors in Dewey's learning process and the way in which it has been extended by American socialization patterns.

Seeing some errors and dangers, we may make some alternative proposals.

John Dewey described "how we think" as a five-step process. While the following five-step summary does some injustice to his esthetics and the subtlety of his thought, it nevertheless captures what was for him the essence of thinking.

1. Thinking begins with a *felt sense* of the problem.
2. The next step is to *formulate* the problem in a conceptually clear, concise way. Dewey's word is "intellectualize."
3. The third step is to *explore* the available *hypotheses* which have a significant bearing on the solution to the problem.
4. The next step is to think "in the narrow sense" about the hypotheses which have suggested themselves, *analyzing* and *elaborating* them.
5. The final step is to bring the product of the first four steps to a testable form and proceed with the *test.*

This description of the thinking process is a general view of inquiry and, in another sense, a view of how we learn through solving problems. Almost everyone can find in himself some basic sympathetic reaction to this sequence which seeks to state summarily the essence of orderly reflection. However, this is not only the supposed procedure for doing ordinary thinking but is also a basic outline for the conduct of scientific research.

The apparent range and significance of this paradigm for inquiry is not confined to its actual application; it also has something of a mystique about it. Dewey's name and this process are central to whatever mystique surrounds the "problem-solving" approach to education. The most striking characteristic of this—not so much in Dewey's original notion but in what it has come to symbolize—is its treatment of affect and the personal achievement of the learner. Between step one and two there is a significant break between the problem as "felt" and the problem as "intellectualized." The solution

(5) is tested out with regard to the problem as stated, *not* the problem as *sensed.* Yet this type of education has been celebrated as involving the learner in the learning process. This can only be said accurately if the learning is dominantly cognitive and the learner wishes to become socialized for affective neutrality. (We will ignore for the moment that, in the extreme, this is the formula for a schizoid experience.)

When one considers the long-range deleterious effect of the educational process which tends to repress affect and stress cognitive problem-solving, the significance of the hiatus between step one and two is quite striking. Consider the oft-quoted article by Urie Bronfenbrenner in which he suggested the dangerous results of stressing "excellence" in the public schools in the post-Sputnik era. Studies he cited observed that, given the contemporary American family and social situation, an educational emphasis upon excellence in the hard, dry sciences to the general exclusion or isolation of dealing with "fantasy and feeling in education" tended to produce students who were more purposeful and planful, but also more tense, domineering, and cruel.

The problem of affect in a context of concern for wholeness in education is not met on the other hand by encounter groups in which the driving aim is to reach gut-level honesty. This is an admirable corrective to a repressive, cognitively dominated situation, but if anything more it tends toward confusing one aspect of a personality (emotions, in this case) with the whole, integrated personality, and calling expression of this onesidedness "honest," "real," and all the other generally dull virtues associated with negative affect. A recent article in *The New York Times* exposed some of the dangers of encounter groups; gut-level honesty can be so gut-ripping that even in competent hands (and frequently encounter groups are not in such hands), the psychic damage may be nearly irreparable, even fatal. But anyone whose concern is for psychic wholeness must, of course, suspect as dangerous from the outset any part-for-the-whole approach to learning.

Kirkegaard once told the tale of the man who escaped from a local insane asylum and headed for the nearby town. As he walked, his pace slackened and he began to sense some consternation. The problem as he formulated it was, "What can I say when I get to the town which will convince everyone that I am sane?" As he puzzled over this problem, suggesting and dismissing several possibilities, he came upon a rubber ball which lay partially hidden in the grass along the road. He picked it up, and as he tossed it up and down he said, "The ball is round, the world is round!" That was it—he would try it. So, he went into the town seizing people and, staring into the whites of their startled eyes, he said with perfect assurance, "The world is round." They put him back in the asylum.

What was said was cognitively sound enough, at least for casual street conversation. Moreover, there was a certain straightforward, no-nonsense aspect to his approach; he was doing his dead-level best to be gut-level honest.

Why did they throw him back in the asylum? Essentially, it was because the two sides of his personality, while appropriate enough in themselves, did not fit together. The integration was missing. He didn't really "get himself together."

This is the content problem of the educational process: how or by what process do we teach and learn integrity of heart? It follows that such a process must be both counter-repressive, if subjunctive life is to be engaged in learning, and cognitively respectable, if it is not to collapse into a "bad trip." The most likely approach to such an integration of cognition and affection is the central core of the creative process, and the factors which foster, sustain, and deepen that process in individuals. It seems to me unnecessary at this point to debate the question of whether or not our educational efforts in a Christian context ought to "put us together"; if wholeness is not more compatible in itself than is a repressively divided psyche with holiness, then it seems to me the burden of proof is on the side of the objector.

In Christian education, then, we are in a search for a coherent perspective on learning which is pragmatic yet does not subordinate personal integrity to either "proper response" or "the gut response." This perspective was suggested quite provocatively in the posthumous work of Harold Rugg, *Imagination*. In the final chapter of this book (which was actually the outline from which Rugg was working before he died), the author set forth the three stages of creative work: the baffled struggle, an interlude in which the struggle is put "out of mind," and then the blinding, unexpected "flash of insight." This blinding flash comes with such certitude that a logical statement of it can immediately be prepared. Extending this to its full length, one can isolate five phases: (1) baffled struggle, (2) interlude, (3) flash of insight, (4) release of tension built up during the struggle, (5) interpretation of the flash, logically relating it to the struggle which preceded it.

Passing through this sequence is both a work of pragmatic power and a process of personal growth. It involves both the familiar language of consciousness—the "logical statement" —and the more intimate but less familiar language of the unconscious—the iconic form of "insight" or "image." The uniting of conscious and unconscious through the unfolding of the creative process is not only a highly erotic experience (not sexy), but also one of heuristic power. In Polanyi's terms, the modification of any anticipatory framework, conceptual or appetitive, is an irreversible heuristic act. The unity of conscious and unconscious in the creative act is a modification of "psychic set"; awareness is expanded, perception is sharpened, the body is suffused with new energy and, as a result, work on the next baffled struggle can proceed at a higher level of complexity. Thus, through the creative process, the hope of coming into a closer touch with reality is enlivened and sustained.

Studies of creativity in social psychology, and particularly in "human information processing," point to the general conditions which foster this process. There are five criteria which contribute significantly to the expression of creative impulses in any learning context. The first is an unwillingness to submit absolutely to any human authority. Authoritarianism is the well-known antithesis to the creative process. Its by-products —traditionalism, superstition, stereotyping, and anti-intraception (a prejudice against taking a long look at what's going on inside)—are designed to preserve established frames of reference by rigid control. Creativity is frustrated from the outset.

The second condition is the only real basis for authority: the recognition and acceptance of personal differences. To put it differently, authority lies in the integrity of each participant, and it is fully in keeping with each one's integrity to respect the probability that disagreements may end not in agreement, compromise, or in one-man-down, but in stable, recognized, and accepted differences. To blur differences to attain what William H. Whyte, Jr., called "group-think," the kind of common denominator group integration which fosters a corporate nincompoop, is to rule out grounds for interactional integrity and, hence, the creative act.

The third condition is a willingness to lay an emphasis upon complexity rather than simplicity in dealing with persons and problems. This requires development of an increasingly high tolerance for ambivalence in persons and ambiguity in cognitive problems. This is not to rule out the simplicity of a parable, for the actual synthesis between human and cognitive factors which signifies the penetrating and informed meaning of the parable is a highly complex matter. In other words, to get the import of a biblical parable is to have the framework of one's natural attitude significantly modified; one does not, *cannot,* look at his world in the same fashion as before. Once wised-up, one cannot wise-down. He must wise-on (assuming that wising-off is out of the question).

The fourth condition is a willingness to have and to bear stress in the course of interaction. The notion of a smooth learning sequence, or growth without conflict, is extremely dubious from the standpoint of any effort to induce and strengthen the creative process. Moreover, the teacher does not learn as he teaches if he will not engage the conflictual struggles which involve the students; students will not learn if they refuse to accept their responsibility to teach each other and the teacher. To expect to resolve issues creatively without stress is to invoke a wide range of naïvete extending from the conforming intellect through socialization patterns to impregnable piety. There are all kinds of ways to avoid stress and remain firmly socialized, but there is no way to do creative learning without a willingness to face and bear with psychic stress.

Finally, the learning context should do everything possible to enable one to trust in his own insight. A recent study showed that a large majority of church school teachers are so preoccupied with the proper conditioned response that they tend completely to ignore or even punish efforts on the part of learners to engage their fantasies and feelings with the content of what is being taught. This is poor learning in any context, but it is a disaster in the context of Christian education where the governing mandate is given by the presence of the teacher/student as a creative person, not by the content of the lesson.

These three sets of five cover a wide variety of demands and situations. If there is a fire, by all means let's follow Dewey to put it out. It won't do to grapple in existential ecstasy over the deeper meaning and personal significance of smoke rising from one's wastebasket. So be it with all situations in which the pragmatic demand is clear-cut. The possibility for personal and convictional growth cannot be delineated by pragmatic conditions. Convictional fires need to be fanned, not dampened; questions of personal and ultimate meaning need —indeed, cry out for—a learning process which, as a process, puts one together as he learns. The five-point creative process does this, but this process in turn cries out for a context which supports, fosters, and develops the process. The last set of five points do this.

Learning which puts a person together is perhaps more a matter of the medium (not the technological apparatus involved, but the human-involvement medium) than it is of the content. But when the content is theological and drives toward connections between holiness and human wholeness, then the content demands a complementary interpersonal medium if the "message" is to connect with the content in moments of insight and convictional growth.

ACTING NOW

A SOCIALIZATION MODEL

BY JOHN H. WESTERHOFF III

The assumptions we make interacting with our experience frame our understanding of education. The questions we ask about education condition the answers we build our educational program upon. To forget these obvious observations is to remain captive to the past. And that's what has happened in Christian education.

It seems as if for a number of years church educators have assumed that their responsibility was to teach people about the content of the Bible, the doctrines and history of the church, and the teachings of Jesus about right and wrong—to introduce people to the Christian religion. Their experience has been almost entirely restricted to instruction in a church-school context. They have tended to think of Christianity in terms of content, the Sunday school and youth groups as the agents of communication and teaching and preaching as the means. The questions they have asked about Christian education have been limited to schooling and so their educational programs have been planned accordingly. Perhaps due to a very different personal history I have often found myself making different assumptions and asking different questions.

The educational model I will attempt to describe in this essay is a result of the interaction of my experience and assumptions. Remember, I had no early experience in a church school and so I never connected Christian education with church schooling. During my graduate years at divinity school, I took only one course which had anything to do with Christian education. It was entitled "The History of Religious Education" and was taught by a member of the faculty at the Graduate School of Education. As I remember, it began with primitive religions and was strongly influenced by anthropology with its focus on enculturation. We concentrated our studies on rituals, institutions, community customs and traditions, myths and symbols. Obviously we also dealt with schooling, but it was always seen as only one aspect of religious education and never the most significant. I also recall being ordained as "pastor and teacher," a charge I took very seriously, thereby seeing education as one of my major concerns. But because pastor was the other half of my vocational commitment I came to see education as being related to worship, counseling, budgets, committee meetings, organizations, and general congregational life. And thus my educational experience provided me with a broad understanding of education. My educational assumptions were influenced by my theological studies which were dominated by biblical form criticism, comparative religions, and the social sciences.

In my biblical studies I came to see that before we can ask what the Bible says we need to ask what the Bible is. And what is it other than a book of poetry, myths, parables, and stories which describe how a community of people with a particular way of looking at the world and history came to be able to discern where love and justice were acting in history and how they might become a community of love, power, and justice in the world? And they learned that as they struggled to become that kind of people.

In comparative religions I came to see that the study of religion by poring over sacred scriptures, history, and theological trends of beliefs and morals was an irrelevant endeavor. Christianity as a religion was unimportant and to know all about Christianity had little to do with being Christian. More important than the religions of men was the faith of men. And faith is how the world looks to a person. It provides the framework of meaning by which the past is understood, the present lived, and the future anticipated. Our faith is our world view; it is the way the world looks to us, and the way we are to live in relation to this world; and it is mediated to us by those with whom we live thereby becoming an integral part of our self-understanding, organizing our lives, directing our actions, and creating our visions.

From the social sciences I learned that men have always thought about the world in which they lived, creating myths about its origin, purpose and future. A world view—faith—is essential for life. Such a world view is communicated to us by a community of faith and the meaning of that faith is very personally developed by each of us out of experiences and actions within and in relationship to that community. We each make sense out of the world and our place in it because a meaningful story of the world is supplied; our experiences interpreted and our actions emerged or discarded by our community of faith. We acquire our world view by observing and doing, following and imitating, experiencing and acting in our community of meaning. That faith is exemplified in a people's distinctive way of life. Education is the holistic socialization process by which that way of looking at life and way of life is purposefully communicated, nurtured, and developed.

No one has faith who has not been in part educated to it by others and yet I always know that my theological studies did not convert me or make it possible for me to acquire my Christian faith. That was done in the context of participation in a local congregation. I remember vividly the experiences I had within such communities and the sense I made out of those experiences as I reflected upon them with others with whom they were shared. I recall the importance of worship: of the pageantry, symbols, architecture, and art; of singing hymns, kneeling and repeating prayers, reading the psalms, reciting the Apostles' Creed, and standing for Gloria Patri and the Gospel. I remember the importance of congregational meetings in which we addressed social issues and planned our corporate action in the light of our faith. I remember joining others in acting out our decisions. In such memorable ways my faith was framed and continues to be enhanced.

Accordingly, I have developed a socialization model for Christian education. But before I describe it, a few remarks on my use of the word model. Typical examples of models in the literal sense of the word might include: a Christmas crèche in a church narthex, an architect's model of the new church school building displayed in a showcase, or a Palestinian village in a church school classroom. That is to say a three-dimensional miniature of some "original" object—a scale model. We also use the word to stand for a type of educational design. For example, a new youth ministry model or the 1970 model Presbyterian curriculum resources. We use the word to mean some example, worthy of imitation: a model church school teacher, a model program of adult education, a model youth celebration, or a new church school model. I do not intend to use the word model in any of those senses, but rather in the scientific sense of an expression of a theory. Currently in Christian education circles the word model is being used a great deal. I suggest that what most people are talking about are educational designs or plans for education which in some sense can be duplicated. They are using the word for the description of something that is or can be occurring somewhere. In a sense, they are describing the application of a theory. Such educational designs are important and helpful. But my intention in this essay is to step back from those designs and attempt to sketch or describe an educational theory—that is, to create a model for Christian education.

My model, like all theoretical models, results from an interaction of my philosophical assumptions on what is (What is knowable? And what is valuable?) with my educational experience. It also gives expression to the influence of particular foundational disciplines—in this case, anthropology and theology.

Obviously, this model cannot be duplicated. It does not offer a concrete proposal or plan for action in any particular educational context. However, numerous and diverse educational designs can emerge from this model. Some of these can be found in the essays which follow in this section. Others can easily be imagined.

The test of a good model is that it helps us to understand our educational experience, it gives concrete expression to our philosophical assumptions, and it enables action in the form of educational designs made operational. For me, the following model does all three.

In my socialization model for Christian education, I focus on three contexts for learning: *Ritual*—meaningful celebration of memory and hope, *Experience*—reflected upon experience in community, *Action*—planned for action around social issues. These three contexts are held together in a dynamic interacting holistic system within the total life of a community of faith. It is a model which attempts to give form to the communication and nurture of the Christian faith through the natural but intentional lifelong processes by which persons in community acquire their world view and way of life. I will attempt to describe each of these contexts separately, although they are obviously always overlapping and interrelating.

Ritual: Meaningful celebration of the memory and hope of our faith. Rituals and liturgies have always been central to the life of the church. Even when every other function of the church has been curtailed its worship has been kept alive. At night in the fields, in the catacombs, in darkened homes the church has kept its faith alive through its rituals. And if the liturgical life is a focal point in the life of the Christian it must certainly be a focal point in Christian education.

Rituals are the deliberate attempt of communities to focus on, communicate and reinforce their way of looking at the world and their way of life—their faith. Rituals provide both the form and occasion for the expression of our Christian faith, a continuing necessary context of Christian education. Through our rituals we celebrate our heritage and tradition, the memory and hope of our faith. It is thus through active participation in ritual action, movement, song and dance that we become aware of the meaning and value of life, our reason for living, and our motives for acting.

Ritual is therefore our first context for Christian education. For too long worship has been estranged from the purview of the educator. The liturgy needs to be seen again as providing a place for deliberate Christian education.

For those who are concerned, as I am, that children come to know our heritage, tradition and the message of the Bible, I suggest that we see the rites of the church as the place for such learning. In the natural meaningful context of our celebrations, we best communicate the memory and hope of our faith.

Such rituals can be divided into two types: rites of solidarity and rites of passage. Rites of solidarity are dramatic community rituals which embrace the sense of the community, identity, and their understanding of the meaning and purpose of life. These rites are celebrated in daily liturgies, the weekly Eucharist and on special occasions, following the liturgical year from Advent to Trinity and including the Saints' days. These rites need to be celebrated in a meaningful environment, an environment which by its very nature communicates the faith. They need to be celebrated, acted out, in meaningful

A SOCIALIZATION MODEL

ways by the whole community—children, youth, and adults. Too often we have dozed through rituals that lack any living meaning and bore children with their meaninglessness. And too often we have remained observers rather than participants at lectures which are passed off as celebrations where drama, music, dance, and participation are called for if the ritual is to have life.

Many of our rites of solidarity will have to be changed, reintroduced or created afresh. Church education should show the way.

A second type of rites are those of passage. These rites celebrate the movement of individuals and the community as they change their status or place in life. For the individual these rites are related to birth, illness, achievement of manhood and womanhood, going away to school or entering the service, graduation, marriage, a new home, a new job, death. They need to give community recognition to the entire complex of new or altered relationships of the members of the community for each has a public implication. For example, many people need to adjust to a birth—the child born, the parents, the other sibling, and the community to which they all belong.

Each rite needs to take all of these facts into account as we participate in meaningful celebrations which address the moment and the need of persons in the light of the memory and hope of our faith.

Rites for the passage of the community need also to be celebrated. For example, New Year's, the Fourth of July, the founding of the church community, the building of a new church, the coming of spring in an agricultural community, the beginning of a school year in a college community, and so forth. Obviously the environment in which these take place and what people do at them needs to be part of these meaningful celebrations of rites of passage.

Through such rituals celebrated in homes, on hilltops and in church sanctuaries the community of faith shapes its life and communicates its way of looking at life and its way of life thereby preparing the community for immediate and future cooperative life and action.

The first responsibility of the church educator is to help the community of faith evaluate what it is now communicating or not communicating about the meaning and hope of its faith. It then needs to help the community plan and act out meaningful celebrations so that this context of its educational ministry can be actualized.

Experience: Reflected upon experiences of the faith. Our faith is expressed in a way of life. We need to experience that way of life to acquire and understand it. Christian faith is fostered and evolved in a community of faith as it attempts to live out that faith.

We need to provide experiences of personal meaning within a community of persons actively struggling to seek the good of others without any thought of personal gain. The educator needs to examine/evaluate the total life of a congregation and plan deliberate opportunities for all persons to experience a style of individual and corporate life which can be characterized as sensitive, responsible, caring for all in need. Unless a person experiences the love and justice which characterizes the Christian life style while participating in the life of a faith community and unless he has opportunities to explore the personal meaning of these experiences *as they occur* he will have missed an important aspect of religious education. Now this does not imply that the church must be a perfect society, but it does mean it needs to be a community of agony and ecstasy within which a person can experience the quest for meaning, justice, and love.

It is as a witnessing community that the church must be understood. The Christian faith can only be communicated by those who participate in a community which is attempting to be a historical agency through which God is making the human world.

Our Christian faith can best be communicated within a community which offers us experiences of persons and groups openly struggling to live out their faith and reflecting upon the experiences they have in the community in the light of that faith. Church educators need to evaluate the kinds of experiences which are being promoted for all persons in the church. They need to plan opportunities for persons to experience a truly living and witnessing community of faith. Among many other contexts such as church suppers, bazaars, and organizations this means also bringing the thinking, feeling, and acting of church boards and committees into the purview of church education. It may mean the establishment of regular congregational meetings set in the context of worship and reflection for children, youth, and adults.

Action: Planned for action around social issues. The words social issues presupposes my theological position that God acts in history as the power of love and justice. To know God and to understand our Christian understanding of life and the role of our lives is to join him in his historymaking. We therefore need to provide opportunities for persons to be involved in the personal and social action of the faith community. That action is, of course, political and economic, but it is just as much pious and devotional. We need to learn to see social action as an instance of prayer and devotion and we need to learn to bring our acts of concern for peace and justice under the humbling judgment of God. We need to learn how to gain the courage and commitment to join him. Little of this will be learned unless we participate with others who are attempting to live in such ways according to such a way of looking at life.

Unless we act out the Christian faith we cannot fully understand it. Until we act out the message of the scriptures—the gospel—in our total behavior: thinking, feeling, acting, it is beyond comprehension. It cannot be our faith if we only talk about it. We therefore need to provide a place where children, youth and adults together are consciously and overtly attempting to act out their faith. And we need to make sure that all our best-motivated actions are evaluated to determine if, in fact, they actually do express our faith. For every idea we profess, an opportunity must be sought to make it real in an identifiable and interpreted action.

The church educator is called upon to help the congregation evaluate its actions and plan opportunities for its members to act out their faith even as they reflect upon the meaning of their actions. Dietrich Bonhoeffer asserted that only in the world is Christ met. Perhaps he was suggesting that we begin our education programs with action groups who go out into the world to meet the needs of the world and who in the context of that action explore the meaning of the Christian faith. This means understanding that while social action and education are distinguishable, they are not separable. Just actions are a result of moral decision-making; that takes practice. But simple participation in action is not education. It is what we do in preparation to act and what we do with our actions to shape them into meaning that can be examined and communicated which makes them educational. What this means is that the church should be seen as a laboratory and training ground to help us learn how to achieve a just social order, how to participate in the formation of social policy, how to make institutions function, and how to engage in corporate action for change. The church educator is responsible for establishing programs in the life of the church which help people to learn such skills and which will help groups to develop those ways of acting which will make them responsible forces in society.

Reflection on the Christian faith only makes sense in the context of experiencing and participating in the life of faith. The Christian life style can only be learned through radical experiments in living. As Ellis Nelson wrote, "We may be approaching a period where the actual and everyday life of the church is the new educational methodology." That's what I am trying to say. And the church educator is the one who sees that "the life of the church" has deliberate purposefulness. Perhaps this implies that the Christian education committee ought to be the central planning body for the church, helping it to make its rituals, experience and action enhance and communicate its faith. To be engaged in these three contexts of holistic socialization is to be engaged in Christian education.

Thus we have a model for Christian education which does not require a school, although it does not rule one out. Surely it is only one of numerous possible relevant models which need to be explored and experimented with, and evaluated by church educators. I offer it not as the answer or panacea for the future, but only as the basis for creating an alternative future for Christian education in the churches.

10
CELEBRATIONS

BY JOHN H. WESTERHOFF III

One night not long ago, I was in the living room of a suburban home near a small West Coast college campus. A young priest in sports clothes had invited me to join him and his congregation for a celebration. These adults, teenagers, and children met regularly to celebrate their common faith and life. A long dining room table was set with loaves of bread and bottles of wine, fruit, and cheese.

The whole house had a festive atmosphere, with colorful paper flowers and birds hanging from the ceiling. I was greeted with a bag decorated on the outside with dayglow letters reading, "We care." Inside was a large red and yellow sheet of tissue paper with a hole in the middle and a variety of other things. We each picked a partner to dress in the paper costume. We read them part of an anonymous poem we had found somewhere: "I love you. You're more valuable than anything in the earth and I like you better than anything in the world."

We fed each other Hershey Kisses. We stuffed a balloon with confetti, blew it up, tossed it in the air, punctured it with a pin. As the confetti fell over us, we blew party horns. The daily news programs blaring from the two television sets in the room were turned down as someone began to strum a guitar. Everyone joined in the folk song "Turn, Turn, Turn" as we made our way to the table.

There, we each greeted our neighbors with the ancient kiss of peace. Everyone had a part in the reading of scripture and in original, brief, simple prayers. We prayed the Lord's Prayer, but following "thy will be done on earth as it is in heaven," reports from the day's newspaper were read. We each made our confession of apathy in the face of need; this was followed by a hug of forgiving affection from a neighbor. An offering of money and fair housing pledge cards was made that evening. Each person made personal affirmations of what he believed. Some were moving. "I believe in God, which is to trust that someone, somewhere, is not stupid." Together we affirmed our understanding of the Christian faith: Where there is life there is death, but where there is death there is hope. We acknowledged that with such a perception of life we could affirm the negative aspects of our times as the birth pangs of a new age.

Our priest broke the bread and blessed it. He poured the wine and blessed it, each person serving his neighbor. We joined hands and sang joyfully, concluding with Jesus' words to Simon Peter, "Simon, son of John, do you love me more than these?" And we answered with Peter's words, "Yes, Lord, you know that I love you." And our host responded as did Jesus, "Feed my lambs."

As we sat at the table to share the bread, cheese, wine, and fruit, we struggled to decide what we must do during the next week in order to make good our celebration in action in the world. Two hours later, as a community, we formulated some definite resolves for action, sang "We Know They Are Christians by Their Love," and with a kiss of peace departed into the night.

All over the country, groups of people are struggling to find more meaningful ways to celebrate their Christian faith. There is a need for all of us to discover significant ways to express our faith by recreating our ceremonies. Such an endeavor is the responsibility of church educators.

Some of my most exciting educational experiences have been with those who wanted to rethink an ancient ceremony in order to give it a contemporary expression. I've also discovered that participation in these is educational in another sense. Add to that the usable moments which arise when participants begin to ask questions and you realize the unlimited educational possibilities related to celebrations.

I remember one evening with two old friends, Bob and Alice. They wanted to celebrate their wedding. This is how it evolved.

They invited twenty of their closest friends to a potluck supper in their back yard. Everyone was also asked to think seriously about his love relationship so he might be able to share some experiences. Alice and Bob spent the morning decorating the yard. They built an open thatched-roof hut of pine boughs and flowers. They hung a bird cage from the roof and moved in a large, flat, crude rock as a table.

The guests arrived. The party began. There was wine to drink and lots of song. Two guests were folk singers who had brought their guitars. Six of the others were in a madrigal group. The ceremony began with music from the past and the present and much joyful conversation. When the couples were ready, they sat down in their hut, called their friends to gather round, and asked me to begin:

Talking seems inappropriate at times such as this, occasions of singing and dancing, of silence and feeling, of celebrating and embracing, of crying and laughing. Bob and Alice, we are happy to be here to celebrate with you formally what already exists—the living love of two who have found joy and meaning together. In a mysterious yet happy way, you bring together two pasts, different in memories, traditions, hopes, and loves. That will not change but will color the future, so that as you become one you will always remain two. That is good. Marriage is not intended to be a melting pot where differences cease to exist, but rather the place where you can be fully and honestly yourself, sharing in the deepest level all that life is and what you are. But before you felt you could publicly express that union and its intentions for the future, you wanted your friends to share their experiences and thoughts.

Most of the guests spoke. Some were single, some divorced, some married. They talked about their experiences, their problems, their joys, their embarrassments, their happinesses, their hurts—everything that went into their lives together and what they hoped would also be Bob and Alice's life.

In this way each person made a pledge of what he would like to do for them. What better gifts could friends bring?

Bob and Alice read some poems to each other. They embraced. They sat by their table and sipped wine together, sharing it with everyone in the group. There were toasts. They took each other's hands and made their pledge:

I give you my hand, I give you my love, I give you myself. I pledge to stand by you as long as we live. Come travel with me and share the hard way, the easy way. I bring this ring forged in love which is to me a symbol of completeness and eternity, and I give it to you to wear so that we will always remember our vows.

The potluck supper was eaten; there was some more singing and dancing. It was a beautiful celebration. People should create their own celebrations. I don't think I could ever return to ceremonies as usual.

I remember another significant adventure in celebration, a baptism that went something like this. The couple whose baby was to be baptized carefully chose from among their friends those who had the same faith, values, life styles as themselves. They invited them to their home and told them to bring party decorations. We entered the living room where the baby was resting in a bassinet. All joined in decorating the room. When we were finished, we sat on the floor in the new, festive environment and sang. The baby seemed to love it. Then we began to talk about the world in which we lived and the world we hoped would someday be. Champagne was passed about and everyone toasted the baby, stating what he was personally going to do on behalf of the baby to help make that vision of a new world a reality. The parents said what they intended to do for their child. Together we knelt around the baby. Water was poured from his baby bottle into a dish, and the parents and I placed our hands in the water and onto the child's head, baptizing him into the faith community. We all joined hands and sang, and the party went on.

Often I have thought we ought to make our celebrations new. Perhaps we also ought to create new celebrations: celebrations for those who decide not to have children, celebrations for those who decide to have children, marriage celebrations, celebrations for those who decide to seek a divorce, celebrations for those who are drafted and for those who refuse to be drafted, for all significant times and events in the lives of people. Even in times of death we can create meaningful celebrations. I remember one. It was different from any funeral I had ever attended, also more meaningful, and exactly as the forty-one-year-old man who had died had wanted it.

His wife and children invited all their friends to the church fellowship hall. When these people arrived, they discovered a room full of card tables and chairs with all kinds of decorating materials scattered about. There was a small combo playing the songs the couple had liked best. As people came in they were greeted by the dead man's wife, who invited them to be merry and find a table where they could talk of what they remembered most about the man who had died. On all the walls were large sheets of white paper. The guests were to decorate these sheets with their memories and anything they would like to celebrate about him. They shared their creations, the band played, people sang, cried, hugged each other, ate, and even made some memorable speeches. As his wife put it, "I've invited you here not so much to ask the question of why he died, but to ask the question of why he lived." Just before the celebration came to an end, each person was given the opportunity to make a toast and a commitment to what he was going to do to make some of his friend's visions and hopes come true, what he planned to do to cause the life of the dead man to continue through his own life. Thus, the resurrection was celebrated and made real in the experience of those who mourned with hope and thankfulness for a life they had loved.

Well, there is an evening sacrament held in a home, a wedding in a back yard, a baptism in a living room, and a funeral in a church social hall. Each of them was created by people to make meaningful their faith in a realistic celebration. The time spent in preparing these celebrations was educational, as were the events themselves. It was a coming together of learning and worship. I'd like to encourage that kind of education in the church, and that kind of celebration.

SHALOM IN POSTMODERN SOCIETY

BY LETTY M. RUSSELL

CHURCH IN CHANGE

The church is in change. There is no question about this. Society is changing rapidly and the church as a part of that society is bound to change. The key question is not: Is the church changing? Nor is it: Is the church changing fast enough to keep up (with the present) or changing too fast to maintain its roots (i.e., tradition)? The key question is whether the church is changing in response to its desire to serve Christ's mission in a relevant way in a postmodern society or simply in reaction to the changes in society. Whether new structures are adaptive to society or contradictory to it, the key question is: Are these structures carefully thought out, worked out, experimented with, and planned, or are they simply a matter of default?

There is much debate today about what a postmodern society looks like among sociologists, educators, futurologists, as well as social reformers, politicians, revolutionaries, flower people, etc. Nevertheless, there is a wealth of data which confronts us all as the various parts of our world speed at various rates beyond the *medieval,* feudalistic, tribal society, and, in

97

turn, beyond the *modern,* technological, nationalistic society. More and more, Western society is moving into another *postmodern,* cybernetic stage of international, intellectualized systems.

In such a world the church needs to develop a variety of forms that will help it to continue in its calling to be a relevant sign of God's shalom. In other periods of history, the church used existing structures such as house churches, dioceses, town meetings, or denominations. Now it must use social structures which are available and suitable to a postmodern society. Because this emerging way of life is one of pluralism (even multiversity), the church is faced with creating relevant, open-ended structures which view institutions as changing and temporary in nature.

One emerging structure, which is especially relevant to the modern period, is the *movement.* A movement is a wide variety of collective attempts to bring about social change. Because it is bound together by generalized goals or ideas rather than a particular structure, a movement makes possible a wide variety of organizational options, both large and small. An example of this can be seen today in what is often called "the underground church movement," or "grass-roots ecumenism." Within this movement are included such things as national "get-togethers," newspapers, social action, pentecostal, liturgical groups which are both above and below ground, and which share a common purpose of subverting the church into becoming a setting for meaningful Christian life style. As a movement, its "goal" is to *contradict* the emptiness, injustice, and inhumanity of the status quo (including the established church).

A second structure which is emerging is that of the *system.* A system is a complex of (interlocking) institutions of a particular society. It is the means by which the interdependent economic-political-educational structures are coordinated in a postmodern society, where the systems are "steered" by computerized technology. A system is not necessarily mono-lithic. It can be set up in such a way as to allow for a wide vari-ety of groupings and opinions. An example of the emergence of such a system is the current planning going on for church union called COCU. This union would make possible the con-solidation of power, resources, money, manpower in such a way that it could be diversified into significant service. The COCU proposal, on paper at least, allows for a great deal of local variety as people seek to address the needs of their par-ticular region in joint action rather than in useless competi-tion. However, it is basically an *adaptive* structure and runs the risk of selling out to the vested interests of the oppressive elements in our society.

A third structure which is already popular and is likely to become more so as the church begins to accept pluralism and change as a way of life is that of the ad hoc group. The ad hoc group, as its name implies, is a voluntary grouping which meets to accomplish a specific and usually limited purpose. Such groups take a wide variety of forms and can be found as part of a movement, or of a system, or as completely inde-pendent of other church institutions. This may become the pri-mary form of the church in the future if it becomes a *diaspora* church—a tiny minority which continues to celebrate the life of Christ in a world of "postreligion" or of "new-religion." An example of this type of ad hoc church is *Shalom, Inc.,* in East Harlem. It would consider itself part of the grass-roots ecu-menical movement, and yet it is also linked to the COCU churches because it is a small, self-supporting, experimental unit of the denominationally supported East Harlem Protestant Parish. It consists of a group of people drawn from East Har-lem as well as other parts of New York City who carry on a va-riety of programs for adults, youth, and children. These pro-grams are designed to make use of the talents of the group in the "business of shalom." They work to create bridges be-tween the artistic world of New York and the youth of East

Harlem through intercultural dramatic and musical programs. Shalom, Inc., is just one of countless ad hoc groups seeking new ways to be signs of shalom in the world of today and tomorrow.

SIGNS OF SHALOM

If the purpose of new forms of church life in a postmodern society is to create and celebrate concrete signs of shalom, it is important to ask: What is shalom? Shalom is a Hebrew word which is described by the writer of Psalm 85 as "love and faithfulness . . . righteousness and peace." To the Hebrews it signified all the possible blessings promised by God to his people. Yet shalom itself defies definition. It is best described as it happens in the lives of men and women. Shalom happens as *harmony among people*. When it does, they are able to tell a story of a particular happening of co-humanity, of community. Shalom happens as *relevant wholeness*. When it does, people find that they are working it out, making it concrete themselves. It is relevant because it is experienced in relation to the lack of wholeness, future, and well-being which confront men in their daily life. Shalom happens as a *gift of hope*. When it happens, it can be celebrated and shared but never possessed or stored up. Perhaps the best way to show the possible ways that a church might be a sign of shalom in a postmodern world is to give an example of the way shalom is celebrated in one ad hoc group which met as part of Shalom, Inc., in the winter of 1969–70. For shalom happens within a group when God's love is felt, shared, and expressed in concrete actions of service and celebration. In this way it becomes a small sign of God's promise of righteousness, peace, and wholeness for all mankind.

CELEBRATION OF LIFE

One of the programs of Shalom, Inc., is that of a group of about twelve people who gather weekly for Bible study and discussion. Approximately once a month the group meeting is devoted to a secular worship service which consists of a potluck supper celebrated as an *agape meal*. This meal is a modern variation of the traditional "love feast" celebrated in the early church as part of the communion in a manner similar to that of the Last Supper. It is a popular form of celebration in grass-roots ecumenical churches because it makes possible a form of intercommunion which is outside the confessional regulations. It can therefore be celebrated by laymen of all confessions without a priest or minister. It is part of the tradition of the church, yet affords an infinite variety of forms which can be used as the group celebrates its own experiences of shalom in a common meal. Thus, at the same time it can be as secular as a cocktail party, as relevant as the lives of those who share together, and as moving as any experience of God's love. Such a meal is a celebration of the life of those who gather to share their experiences. It is also a celebration of the life of Jesus Christ, which life makes possible hope for all mankind.

This celebration first of all reflects the variety of *service* (*diakonia*) rendered by the group as it gathers. This particular group sees as its purpose the breaking down of barriers between the subcultures of an urban society. There are nuns, ex-nuns, ministers, students, businessmen, teachers, welfare recipients, performing artists within the group. The people are both rich and poor, black and white, American and non-American. There are frequently visitors from the Third World, from the addict community, from Black Power groups, from other experimental groups and communes. When in the liturgy the bread is broken and the wine poured for peace and hope for mankind, this group is celebrating God's concern for that new mankind, a concern which has been acted out in their individual daily lives, in their service to East Harlem through Shalom, Inc., and in their gathering together to celebrate the gift of shalom.

Second, the celebration represents the concern of the group to *discern* God's action in the world. This gift of discernment (*diakrisis*) is a gift of God's Spirit (1 Corinthians 12:10). Christian communities are called to reflect critically on the events of the world, for they are called to criticize society in the light of their hope in God's promise. Many times the meetings take place in moments of crisis and despair concerning our national and international life. Yet in reflecting on the message of the Bible and their own lives, these people seek out ways to "account for the hope that is in [them] (1 Pet. 3:15)." This action of discernment is reflected in the liturgy in its "concerns of the world" when the group talks for as much as an hour on the particular topic for the evening and then toasts *shalom* to all those who stand in particular need of God's blessing and for those who in even small ways have received blessings of happiness and joy which can be shared. You can be sure that last year there were many joyous toasts for the New York Mets, and agonizing toasts for Biafra and Cambodia, as well as countless other more specific and personal toasts.

Last, the celebration represents the joy of this small community as shalom happens in its midst. For, above all, the agape meal is designed as an *anticipation* (*prolepsis*) of the gift of God's shalom to all men. It is, in fact, the celebration of life in God's kingdom now, a small enactment of the messianic banquet when "Many will come from east and west and sit at table . . . in the kingdom of heaven (Matt. 8:11)." The people in the group are committed to bringing God's will for peace and justice to mankind *now* through their actions, and here they celebrate that commitment as they remember in the liturgy that this simple meal of fried chicken, tuna casserole, etc., is the sign that in God's eyes the "war is over," his victory is sure. Thus, together they celebrate not only life as it has happened, and is today, but life as the reality of God's future for mankind. They celebrate and go forth with the kiss of peace or handshake of fellowship to continue their ministry of shalom in God's world.

AD HOC LITURGY

This liturgy, which is quoted as an illustration of "celebration of life," is not a set pattern. It is only one of many possible patterns which are available to a group of Christians who gather to celebrate their life and the gift of Christ. The most important characteristic of this ad hoc liturgy is that it is *not sacred*. It can all be changed and should be shaped by any group which wishes to express its freedom to develop its own style of life. Such groups have the Bible and the symbols of freedom, life, and peace. They can and will work out their own celebration of shalom in postmodern society. Shalom!

SHALOM LITURGY

INVITATION: Isaiah 25:6–9 (paraphrased)

Leader: On the holy mountain the Lord of all power will prepare a banquet for all peoples, a feast of superb
wine, of delicious food.

All the people cannot see things as they really are;
they have, as it were, a veil before their faces;
these veils will be destroyed;
their "ideologies" will be done away with.

He will be victorious over death, forever!
The Lord God, he will wipe away tears from all
eyes.

He will make it come to pass that even his people
will no longer be a scandal on the face of this
earth. . . .

People: LOOK HERE, NOW, *THIS* IS WHAT WE MEAN BY
"GOD"! WE HAVE WAITED FOR HIM, HOPING THAT
HE WOULD LIBERATE US;
AND *THERE* HE IS, THE LORD. WE HAVE WAITED
FOR HIM.

NOW LET US BE GLAD AND CELEBRATE HIS LIB-
ERATION!

All: OUR FATHER, WHO ART IN HEAVEN . . .

BLESSING OF THE BREAD AND WINE:
Leader *(as he breaks the bread):* The bread of peace for all
mankind.
People: THANKS BE TO GOD.
Leader: The wine of hope poured out for all nations.
People: THANKS BE TO GOD.
Sing: SHALOM (Peace) A Hebrew round sung by ecumeni-
cal groups in Europe and the United States. (Words
vary to fit the occasion; music to *Shalom, No. 11*
found in RISK, New Songs for a New Day, Vol. II, No.
3, 1966.)
Shalom, break the bread,
Shalom, pour the wine, Shalom, Shalom.
He's with us today
To show us the way, Shalom, Shalom.

Shalom, my friends,
Shalom, my friends, Shalom, Shalom.
We answer Christ's call
Of service to all, Shalom, Shalom.

Shalom, King of Kings,
Shalom, Lord of Lords, Shalom, Shalom.
He's King of the world,
The Lord of us all, Shalom, Shalom.

EATING OF THE SHALOM MEAL (talking, singing, and eating
together):
Leader: "Many will come from east and west and sit at table
with Abraham, Isaac, and Jacob in the kingdom of
heaven" (Matthew 8:11).

All: SHALOM.

CONCERNS OF THE WORLD:
Report of events that are of concern to the community for intercession and thanksgiving. (Here Bible, newspaper, record, poem, discussion, etc. may be used.)
Toasts of peace (Here toasts of Shalom should be made for the concerns of intercession, thanksgiving, and celebration.) At the end of each toast the speaker says "Shalom," and all respond, SHALOM.

LITANY (repeat each line after the leader):
Say it loud!
Say it clear!
For the whole world to hear!
God is not dead.
God is bread. God is bread. God is bread.
God is bread for North Vietnam and bread for South Vietnam.
Bread for Israel and bread for the Arab World.
God is bread for the poor and bread for the rich.
Bread for the black, bread for the white.
God is bread.
Bread of peace, broken for all mankind.
Wine of hope, poured out for all nations.
The nations will come to God's banquet.
Soon, the nations will come.
All nations are already on their way.
For the war is over.
Listen, the war is over.
Hey, listen folks: The war is over!
Shalom. Shalom. Shalom. Amen.

HANDSHAKE OF FELLOWSHIP.

12 THE OPEN CHURCH SCHOOL

BY FRANCES W. EASTMAN

"Are we all set?" asks the husband half of the husband-and-wife team who are supervisors of Union Church's new experiment with the open classroom approach.

The group of seven adult leaders look carefully at a sheet of newsprint posted on the wall before them. It reads:

Objective: the children will have experiences which help them identify forgiveness and reflect on it.

"That's what we decided at our planning session last week. And we've set up the interest centers for our activities accordingly," says one of the group. "We'd better be all set!"

The group gathered in a small room adjoining a large twenty-by-thirty-foot classroom. They begin to move into the larger room. "In case another real-life situation occurs this morning, I hope we can really help the kids," observes another. "As an enabler, I'm definitely on the learning side of things."

Most of the leaders busy themselves at one of the activity centers. Two stay near the door. As children begin to arrive, adults help them find their name tags on the pinup board and invite them to choose what they want to do. "Feel free to move around among the activities," is the word. The children come in assorted sizes and shapes—from ages six to eleven, with all degrees of shyness and self-assurance. This is only their second Sunday in the new open classroom church school.

In one corner of the room, set off by two screens, a table with clay stands invitingly. Lively, joyous music comes from a record player stationed on a second table. A bright-colored placard mounted by the screened entrance reads: USE THE CLAY TO SAY HOW YOU FEEL WHEN SOMEONE HAS FOR-GIVEN YOU . . . OR WHEN YOU ARE IN NEED OF BEING FORGIVEN . . .

In another corner, a table holds a multiple-jack tape cassette listening set. Another bright placard invites children to listen to a story that Jesus told about a son who needed forgiveness and what his father did. Another cassette recorder with a microphone invites students to record their own story about people forgiving each other. A second-stage part of the same corner offers a puzzle game: events in Jesus' story are lettered in small segments on colored tags; the student is to arrange them in sequence. Stage three of this activity center provides for small-group informal dramatization of the story. Costume materials and props are available, with an enabler to help students work out their dramatization. Glove-type hand puppets and a storybook about contemporary children who have a hard time getting with forgiving offer a fourth optional activity in this setting.

Floor-length windows form one wall of the room, with a courtyard beyond. A table of embroidery materials stands in front of them. Colored burlap, yarn, and needles are laid out; a large piece of burlap hangs on an easel. The placard reads: MAKE YOUR OWN SYMBOL FOR FORGIVENESS AND PUT IT ON OUR BANNER.

In another corner, an overhead projector with transparen-cies and drawing materials stand at one end of a table. At the other is a filmstrip projector with a supply of several filmstrips and recorded scripts. Placards suggest that children look at the filmstrips about Jesus and listen to the scripts, then tell their reactions by making a transparency and projecting it.

Easels and paints for painting HOW YOU FEEL WHEN YOU HAVE FORGIVEN SOMEONE stand in a fourth corner. In the center of another wall a placard says, COMPOSE A SONG AND SET THE WORDS TO MUSIC. Simple flute-type recorders, paper and pencil, and a skilled musician-enabler are part of this center. A large round resource table in the center of the room holds picture and story books, Bibles, pictures, paper, and pencils.

As the children enter the room, some of them skip. Others walk slowly and look around cautiously. Others just stand and look for a while. Each at his own pace, boys and girls are permitted to find the activity of their choice. For the diffident, a leader makes a suggestion or two, then steps back and lets the child decide. One boy, obviously retarded, settles at no center but wanders from one to the other, stopping occasionally to say something to a leader. Finally he settles at the easel and paints picture after picture. The wife half of the supervisory team mounts each of his paintings on the wall as he finishes and sits down to keep him company.

Elsewhere, two eager beavers collide vociferously over use of the filmstrip projector. A leader joins them and a three-way discussion of a filmstrip on "The Prodigal Son" eventually gets under way. Then one boy works on a transparency while the other struggles with dictating the words of a song to the musician-enabler.

At times, one center is overpatronized. When too many boys engulf the embroidery symbol center, two leaders work with the group, talking about forgiveness and what the students want to say. While some of the boys sketch symbols, others use needle and yarn. When any center momentarily has no business, the assigned leader engages himself in work. No adult stands around doing nothing.

So activity ebbs and flows. The room hums at a happy noise level. Voices, records, thumping clay, flute notes—all mingle without creating distraction. Toward the end of the period, notes on a sarna bell gong remind the children that the time to join other classes for a closing worship period is approaching. Union Church also conducts classes on traditional lines, and all children join for worship.

The worship time concluded, the teachers in the open classroom gather for a brief evaluation. They will meet again on Monday evening for their weekly planning session. None of them likes to miss it, for they are discovering genuine community and fellowship in their common concern for helping children become involved in the life of the church.

Union Church's version of the open classroom approach is only one instance of the way in which this free, flexible setting for teaching/learning may be used in the church's educational work. There can be almost as many variants as there are situations using it, since each church should adapt fundamental principles to its own local situation. The open classroom may incorporate a broadly graded setup, such as Union Church's ages six to eleven, or a less broadly graded arrangement such as grades one through three or four through six. This approach may also be used successfully within a more closely graded setting, such as with children in grades one and two, three and four, or five and six—or with children of a single-age classification. The approach to teaching/learning is the keynote.

Some of the fundamental characteristics of the open classroom approach are:

1. Teaching/learning is a joint enterprise between adult leader (enabler) and students. The program is geared to give the student the power of choice of the learning activities he wishes to pursue. Leader-enablers are present to assist and offer guidance to the students and to be of help to them in doing their own learning.

2. Session structure is based upon goals and objectives which are chosen in advance. Themes and procedures for implementing them are selected from curriculum and other resources coupled with evaluation and student feedback from previous sessions.

3. Activity or interest centers related to the themes are planned for use by individuals and/or small groups. The types of possible experiences usually feature discovery learning coupled with instruction and interpretation.

4. Students move freely from center to center at their own pace in the process of personal discovery and learning.

5. Leader-enablers assist students in whatever ways are required. These may include management of the activity materials, interpretation of the theme or resource materials, talking with students as person to person, listening—always endeavoring to enter into a genuine relationship with the student but not to dictate his course of action. Whenever leaders are not directly engaged in working with a student, they participate actively at a center on their own level, keeping alert to what is going on in the entire classroom, since leaders may also move from center to center if needed. A leader is usually needed to keep in touch with "happy wanderer" students who do not settle down at any center, or with the rambunctious types who may charge about the room, seeking to keep them in touch with the group or helping them work through their private agenda.

6. A large room offers the best facilities for an open classroom approach, but large rooms may be achieved in various ways if church architecture tends otherwise. For instance, an old Akron-plan situation can be used to great advantage, with the open center space as a place for resources, activities requiring free movement, and group gatherings, while the "cubby holes" provide space for activities such as record-listening, drawing, music-making, and the like. Or hallways adjacent to medium-sized rooms may be used as an open class-

room extension to provide space for additional activity centers.

The open classroom approach is one form among several flexible, learning-centered styles of carrying on church education which are being experimented with by churches. Where careful planning, adequate goal-setting, and sound preparation have been provided, adults and children alike rejoice in the exciting sense of accomplishment and community that results. Faith and heritage come alive at the same time that human beings also come alive and discover themselves, the church, and new dimensions of living in the process. The United Church of Christ's Division of Christian Education has drawn up a brochure based on a model of this approach. It is entitled *The Learning Center Approach: Guidelines for Understanding, Planning and Utilizing It in Church Education.* Forms of the learning center approach include open classroom, thematic activity, community-building, and self-instruction, and are described in the brochure. An interpretive slide set with tape cassette accompanies the *Guidelines.*

13
LEARNING SPACE FOR A LEARNING COMMUNITY

BY JOHN M. LARSEN

One Sunday morning Greg, a kindergartener, walked into our Learning Community at The First Congregational Church in Everett, Washington and announced, "I have a new baby sister. She's a week old. She's in the cribroom."

Christy, a young mother with two children of her own, was busy playing with some preschoolers in one corner of the room. At Greg's announcement she stopped what she was doing and told the other children about Greg's new role of being a big brother. Greg joined them. Some of the children who had small brothers and sisters told how they didn't like their change of status in their families. They expressed how they felt when the baby took a lot of their mother's time which they wanted. It was important for them to share their feelings with others. After some discussion of what responsibilities and joys were involved in such a new status, Greg led Christy and the group of children to the nursery so they could all see the tiny bundle that had changed him from being an only child in his family.

When the group returned to our Learning Community room, they spent the rest of the morning in discussion and celebration. Our Learning Community is a place where learning experiences like this can happen, and many other things as well. We began three years ago by asking what kind of Christian we wanted in our church and what kind of program and learning environment would best meet that objective. Ever since, we have been building a new kind of educational program. We call it our Learning Community.

A member of our church admitted: "It hasn't been easy to free ourselves from preconceived ideas of what a church school should be like, but we've kept at it." That kind of determination helped us plan an imaginative program and a new "one-room school." That wasn't easy. No one could conceive of a learning community or a church school without individual classrooms for each age group.

To rethink our educational program, we turned to the children. The young children wanted a place to play, the third-graders wanted a place to make things, and the sixth-graders wanted a place to discuss questions. Some third-graders, however, wanted to study and talk quietly. Some sixth-graders wanted to build things. A number of children said they didn't want to go to church school by themselves. They wanted to be with their parents. A teacher said, "You have to remember that every child doesn't learn in the same way." I said, "Our program and building must be a reflection of the life of a people, the family of God's people who join together for celebration, learning, and service."

When we began our Learning Community we aimed first to create a learning environment. Everything in our building was to have educational value. For example, we created an aviary to change a liability into an asset. A large window well with steel grating over the top let the only outside light into an old room which we had to use. We covered it with fiberglass and built it into a home for a large number of parakeets and cockateels. The birds have now become an important learning resource for both children and adults.

The Sunday a bird died one adult assumed the responsibility of helping the children deal with death. It was obvious that the experience of death meant different things to different children. He asked, "What should we do with the dead bird?" The children responded, "Let's skin it and make a rug."

"You can't make a rug from a bird. You have to make a hat from a bird."

"Let's let him lay over there in the corner."

"We can't do that. It will get smelly in the room."

"No it won't. The other birds will take care of him."

"Let's bury him."

"Then who will take care of him?"

"God will."

Tradition finally triumphed, and the bird was buried in the garden. They wrote their own funeral ceremony and some bits of the new landscaping greens were sacrificed to mark the grave.

Other questions about death which surfaced during the creating of the ceremony were the difference between sleeping and death, and the relation of illness to death. The children learned from the experience, but we all learned that conversation with children about death is important and meaningfully possible. This discovery became crucial when a few weeks later five-year-old Arlene had to be told that her parents were dead following a tragic automobile accident.

There were other days when the birds made it possible, probably necessary would be a better word, for everyone to examine other aspects of life.

A green parakeet hen had her second family for the summer. Everyone was looking forward to the time the new babies would climb out of the nest box. Then one Sunday morning we looked in the nest box only to discover that another hen had fought the green hen for possession of the nesting place. The green mother hen was dead. Everyone was afraid that the babies would die because there was no way to feed them.

Then it was discovered that a blue bird had adopted the babies and was feeding them until they were able to care for themselves.

There was no effort made to moralize to the children on the events. It was not necessary. The children were able to see what had happened and their conversation showed us that they were learning about the suffering which results from uncontrolled rage.

On another Sunday we discovered that one of the beautiful blue baby birds had a birth defect and would not be able to fly. We discussed this with the children, and it was decided that the bird would have to be removed from the aviary to make sure it was not injured by the other birds. As a result, permission was granted to one girl to take it home, with the agreement that she would bring it back from time to time for everyone to play with.

While opportunity to gain biblical knowledge is available in our Learning Community, there is no anxiety about giving the children large amounts of such knowledge. It is determined by their own interest and questions. When a circumstance arises that a child wants to learn something about the Bible, we attempt to translate that concern into our own day. For example:

Tom is in the fifth grade and a confident, outgoing boy. He loves to participate in drama. Together with his friend, Bill, they decided to plan and present a drama of the story of Noah which they had been read at home by their parents. One Sunday, after they had built an ark with others from some material on hand, they wrote their play and presented it—much to the delight of both the children and adults present.

This time they took the parable of the good Samaritan. For their cast they decided upon two people they thought should help you if you need help. They decided on a baby sitter and a Boy Scout. Now they needed someone they would never expect to help. They decided upon a girl their age.

The boys recruited friends to help with their drama. Their

friends proved to be a poor choice. They all ended up leaving for other projects. Alas, this drama never was staged.

In John Westerhoff's book, *Values for Tomorrow's Children,* he talks about individualism in the American church. He makes the case that individualism needs to be addressed or we will not be able to deal satisfactorily with our social problems. I say people need to learn to work together. Often people ask me, "Will our Learning Community help children learn to be churchmen who can work together on solution of our social problems or only unrelated individuals who do their own thing?"

In our Learning Community program, we believe children learn that cooperative effort with their peers and with adults is necessary if they are going to be able to do the things they want to do. Concern for people, the environment, our animals and birds are all part of our learning climate.

A housewife, whose own children are grown and now have families of their own, comes to the Learning Community each Christmas time to help the children make goodies to be taken to shut-ins in Everett. One year it was jelly, another candy. Frances takes several days for the distribution of the goodies because she has the children who made them join her in delivering them. There is always time to stop to talk a little. One girl in the fourth grade reported, "The old people are real nice and they seem awful glad to see us. One lady kissed every one of us."

In recruiting adults to work in our Learning Community, an effort is made to make use of each person's skills or knowledge. In this way we encourage our members to share a part of themselves with children. A very rich source of such leadership can be found in the older members of our congregation. As they participate with the children and share their experiences, the children begin to recognize the values by which these older people live.

Let's take a look at how this works. Mabel is about five feet tall, a lovely person with a radiant personality and a keen zest for living. During her more than four score years (I would not be indelicate enough to ask her exactly how many), she taught school inspiring both her students and contemporaries. Her summers were spent as a fire warden, in solitary vigil on top of an isolated mountain peak. But she never allowed this pioneering effort as the first woman to hold such a position to be written up. She was afraid that calling the state bureaucracy's attention to the fact they had a female fire warden on a lookout high in the Cascade Mountains might bring her summer career to an end.

One Sunday morning, Mabel volunteered to come to talk with any children interested. When the children arrived, there was some music and singing in one corner of our large open "classroom." Then the leader announced the activities for the day. One opportunity was to be conversations with Mabel.

"Today, in the conversation corner, Miss McBain will be happy to talk with you. She used to be a teacher at Everett High School and if your parents went to Everett High, maybe you can find out how much trouble they got into in school. What she is here to talk about are her experiences at a forest lookout tower. She was the first woman to do that. Those of you who like to hike in the mountains will also want to ask her about some of the best trails." During the hour numerous children dropped by for a chat.

Of course, from time to time problems come up. These are resolved by the youth and adults present on that particular Sunday. One Sunday a group of fifth- and sixth-grade boys gathered in the boys' restroom "to get away from the girls." Pretty soon it became necessary for them to make sure the girls knew they were able to get away from them so they developed a game of running out to tease the girls and run back to the boys' room. This was disruptive to the extent that it became necessary for something to be done. One of the mothers went in the boys' restroom and told them to come out and stop their game.

In our postsession evaluation it was decided that boys sometimes need to be able to get away by themselves. In the future it was decided that the men would join the boys and try to redirect their energies. To celebrate that decision, one of the youth painted a picture on the restroom wall of Snoopy dancing for joy. Over his head it says, "Happiness is a place where girls can't go."

Another week, when the same behavior began, one of the men talked with the boys and they decided to build a club house with no girls allowed. They built it in the big room. The girls wanted to build one of their own. But they wanted some boys to help them. In the process, the boy's club was dismantled to use the material for the new construction, and as a result of working together the segregated club project was abandoned in favor of a community center.

Adults and youth share their hobbies and skills with children. One man brought in his scuba gear to show the children why he enjoys diving. An optometrist showed the children how he examines eyes and a doctor brought in a stethoscope. When the chief of police talked about his job some of the boys were so interested that the next Sunday he arranged for squad cars to take the children to the police station.

Our Learning Community needs only one large room, half-carpeted and half tile. In the center is a large fountain which has an aquarium built in it and a place to wash your hands as well. The equipment in the big room will vary from Sunday to Sunday, depending upon what is planned. Right now, we have a large paper-mache turtle that the kids made as one project and a boat which the kids play in and use for great sailing adventures around the world. In one corner is the painting area and all the art work is displayed across the back wall of the room.

A listening area is provided. It is made up of two cassette recorders and numerous earphones. Here the children can listen to tapes as well as make their own.

In an adjoining room are the toys (housekeeping equipment, dress-up clothes, etc.) which appeal to smaller children.

Each Sunday children from three years of age through sixth grade come to enjoy the Learning Community while high school youth and adults come to act as leaders or enablers. Prior to Sunday, the leaders—anyone in the church from junior high school age or older—meet with our part-time associate minister and the Christian education committee, which is responsible for arranging for Sunday morning. They plan a variety of learning opportunities for Sunday.

As children and youth arrive in this one large room, they put on name tags found on a large bulletin board and roam around the room to see what has been planned for the morning's smorgasbord of activities. Everyone is called by his first name. High school youth sit in a corner playing guitars. People enter, gather about them, and begin singing folk songs together. Short announcements by each interest leader explain what the choices for Sunday are. Then everyone is off. Some go to a single activity and remain for the whole hour. Others roam from activity to activity. Some just drift and watch. Anything goes. A group could make jelly or bread, or stomp grapes to make wine for communion. Only imagination limits what might happen on any Sunday. The Christian faith might not be discussed but it certainly is being experienced and acted upon. From my point of view, that's the primary goal of church education.

Various kinds of pets visit the Learning Community from time to time. When Brad and Chris had a pet lamb they thought it very natural to bring it to the church and share the enjoyment of playing with it with the other kids. On other days there have been ducks, puppies, and even a very large pet python.

Ted works with the 4-H clubs of the county and had one of our girls bring in her dog which she was raising to be trained as a guiding dog for a blind person. On successive Sundays we had a blind man visit us with his dog to show the children how the dog helped him get around. We also had a film showing how puppies are raised and trained for this purpose available for those interested.

The Learning Community is planned to accomplish some of the goals of Christian education. In the early years, we try to give children an experience of relationships in the church best described as a loving fellowship. Experience is the key to our Learning Community. The junior high school years are used to reflect upon that experience in the light of our faith and heritage. Our senior high confirmation program aims to help individuals face the implication of their experience in terms of a decision to engage actively in the life of the church. Following confirmation, the youth are encouraged to work in the Learning Community as well as engage in other parts of church life.

One Sunday Russell was pretty destructive. He tried to break down a house some other kids had made and in general created a number of problems. Dan, a high school senior, was asked to work with Russell and see if he could find out how to help him. That evening at the youth meeting Dan talked about the experience. He said Russell had trouble finding things to do; when he had a friend to play with things were just fine. In fact, Russell had become so interested in running the projector that he did not notice when the hour was over. When asked if he found it hard to work with Russell, Dan said, "No, it's not work. It's just interpersonal relations. It's neat." They decided to have each of them take a week as Russell's special friend until he felt at home and good about himself so he wouldn't need to get attention by breaking other children's creations.

It has become obvious to us that the experience of working with the children means a lot to the high school young people. They make no effort to hide the affections they feel for the children. For example, little Greg was new to the Learning Community and Cindy, one of our youth, was thrilled by the artistic ability of this little boy. Most Sundays he spent quite a bit of time with this high school girl who prepared his paints and helped him get started with his favorite project. One Sunday he painted a special picture for Cindy. She took it home and hung it on the wall of her room. She reflected on her relationship with Greg, then wrote:

Child
With deep blue eyes
He looks up at me
Trust and admiration
Radiating from his confident smile
We learn from each other
He and I
I do my best to teach him
How to love all people
And have concern
For others
While he is making me realize
How much I need other people
And he is showing me
All the love I have for humanity
And makes me love it more
Just by looking up at me
Through those deep blue eyes.[1]

We think this is real Christian education. It is hard to describe but when it happens, it is easy to recognize.

Here, in our one-room Learning Community, children, youth, and adults learn together according to their interests. Children learn from each other and with youth and adults in ungraded situations. We improvise the curriculum. The content is the method. We are not anxious to pour information into children's heads. The community is the message in the church. We are trying to find a way to live that community and its memory, which is the Christian fellowship, within the school of the church.

Our congregation is trying to break free of past patterns and discover new ways to fulfill the church's educational ministry. We don't know exactly where we are going. We have more questions than answers, but our dream is to eliminate the old church idea and provide an opportunity for the whole church to gather each week and live together. That's a learning community. But it lives within what we have built into a learning environment. The need for such an environment for a truly meaningful learning community was again impressed upon me a few years ago when I went to speak at a neighboring church.

The request said, "Talk to our Couple's Club about Christian education." But when I walked into the church, it appeared obvious that there was some gap between my expectations and theirs. In response to a whispered question, my wife estimated the average age of those present to be seventy-two-and-one-half years. Surely, my prepared speech on religion and child development within the family was not going to make sense. My solution was to improvise a new subject.

I began, "Tonight I'd like to suggest that we take a look at the life of children in the church. To do this I'd like us to talk about our childhood memories of the church." The first response went like this: "I don't want to say where this church was, but I do want to tell you about how we used to get to where the children met. You walked in the front door, turned to the right, and went downstairs. The treads were wooden and very worn. In the basement you crossed a room to the far corner. Our space was beside the furnace."

As the evening progressed, people described things like the color of the chairs, the smell of the room, and the appearance of the tables. No one mentioned what he was told. Each of their memories had to do primarily with space and experiences within that space.

That evening, combined with a lot of other discussions with people of various ages, has convinced me that the space where learning experience occurs is one of the most important aspects of education in the church, an aspect we often ignore.

For me, the learning climate in a church is related to the appearance of the steps, the paint, the shape of the walls, and the smell of the room. These physical factors teach children about the nature of the church and what the church believes about people. Too often, we have tended to think that children learn what they are told. But even a modest reflection upon our own learning will convince us that it is what we experience that is most important to us.

An educational building of cubicle-like classrooms suggests that experience here will be limited to small groups in isolation from others. Chairs set in even rows suggest that children are expected to be immobile. Decorating to the tastes of the women's guild suggests that this space is not for children except insofar as they are guests.

There are people who feel that the above messages are what they intend. Needless to say, then, their facilities are consistent with their goals for education. I don't happen to agree, but this is the reason that, even at the risk of belaboring the obvious, I believe the first requirement of Christian education is the establishment of goals and purposes. Only then can we discuss the learning space which will be consistent with our intentions.

Our major concern should be to make our learning space

as we do our beliefs. Once we are clear on that, we might evaluate carefully our church and its use of space.

Recently, I worked with a group of enthusiastic young parents who wanted to consider how their educational plant could better serve their children's needs. They were faced with one problem: the building was almost new and there could not be any extensive changes.

We began our analysis by entering as most children would from the parking lot, and we tried to put ourselves in the place of those children. The door from the parking lot was a back door—and looked it. When you entered you found yourself on a landing between two floors with no indication where you should go. When you got to the bottom of the stairs, there was a door straight ahead. We opened the door and were in a storage closet. Backing out, we followed the hall to the next corner. There we found double doors on the right and the hall turned left. The double doors led to a large room with tile floor, high concrete ceilings, and cement block walls. The colors were white and tan with a bright spot of color over the door. The spot of color said: "No Smoking."

When we backed out and followed the long hall, it turned out to be a traffic way between two rows of rooms. The ceilings were twelve to fifteen feet high and made of precast concrete. Light from the outside came through window wells that were some eight feet above the level of the floor. It was impossible to look out the windows.

We concluded that this was not the sort of learning space we wanted, but the problem was this: What could be done to increase the usability of this building and create a better learning climate? First, we wanted to create a new, inviting point of entry where children would have no fear of being lost. We wanted to redesign our buildings so that children would feel at home. One way, we discovered, aimed at appealing to their sense of sight. For small children, who cannot read, we could design pictures that indicate which way they should go, or we could put footprints on the floor and thereby create a fun path for them to follow. And murals could be painted on the wall to create easily recognizable landmarks.

We also talked about appealing to their sense of hearing, since children often mention the scary feeling of being in a church alone due to its silence. We thought of a fountain at the foot of the stairs to give the sound of happily gurgling water. Fish in the fountain might also give a visual feeling of life.

We decided to move the educational program from the small rooms to the large room where we could meet on an un-graded basis. In order to make this large open space a more effective learning climate, we decided to strengthen visually the center of the room. We wanted to create an effect which would invite children into the room.

Some parents designed a large and very attractive aviary for the middle of the room. It was in the shape of a cross, so that a person had to walk into the room and around it in order to see it all. We found that children hurried into the room to be near the birds. The sounds of birds helped strangers find the area and the happy sounds that issued forth created a sense of expectancy.

I have a suspicion that there are a number of other ways in which these live birds or other pets add to the learning cli-mate. A child who comes into the strange new climate of the church is often afraid. Seeing these animals diminishes some of his anxiety. Children can understand that if people love and care for birds here it is probably a pretty safe place for little boys and girls.

Because this large room was not sufficient to hold all the children, we needed to find an imaginative way to use the small rooms as well. We first turned the hall into a city street, with banners hanging from the ceiling to make a feeling of joy and mark the space as belonging to them. This treatment also lowered the high, awesome ceiling, so the children felt at home. They made the banners so the space now belonged to them. "That's the banner I helped make, Mom."

We turned the large classrooms into interesting shapes. A large bulletin board outside each room provided a great place to display some of the children's work. It also gave an idea of the many fun things children could learn and do. The rooms inside became arranged and decorated for the particular activity carried out there. Now there could be free movement throughout the children's space.

All of this wasn't perfect, but it was economical. It also created the kind of space that the church wanted for their children, space the children themselves helped to create, space that could help them learn about our faith. It's easy once you start thinking about it. Get some adults, some high school youths, and some little kids together and start to dream about what you might do in your church. Each dream will help move the thinking of all of you a little closer to what your learning climate should be. All of a sudden—it will be fun! Then you are there. You are creating a climate for learning.

14
SUBURBAN ACTION

BY CHARLES C. LEMERT

In the early sixties, curriculum writers began to take note of the urban world and the problem of racism. Suddenly, in grade-school readers, a black-faced Billy or Mary appeared in pastoral, suburban backyard scenes. These tokens were a cautious and polite beginning, but neither the publishing industry nor Madison Avenue got to the guts of the issues.

This gentle introduction has given way to a more fundamental reformulation of curriculum materials. Today, more and more church study programs are organized around urban problems or the life of Martin Luther King, Jr. Public schools are gradually scheduling courses in Negro heritage and field trips into urban areas. Change is underway.

However, we need to continue this progress by adding another phase. We have demythologized the smug, WASPish postwar study materials by focusing on inner-city problems. It is now time to reconstruct educational thinking in terms of the social problems created by suburban life.

This will not be easy. Suburbia presents special problems for curriculum writers. There are no dramatic human symbols, like Martin Luther King, Jr., or Malcolm X. There are few disturbing pictures of social disease, such as rotten housing or riots or demoralizing unemployment. No brightly wrapped packages of poverty statistics can be used to titillate moral indignation. In sharp contrast to the ghetto community, the suburban community is visually and imaginatively bland. The colorlessness of suburbia is a problem for social activists, responsible churchmen, and forward-looking curriculum writers.

The suburban malaise has been under considerable discussion since the fifties. There has been a verbal overkill by critics who rail against suburbia's conformity and shallowness. The indignation and defensiveness of suburbanites seem to confirm the general accuracy of this criticism. But much of the controversy over the merits of suburbia has been misplaced. The basic fact about the suburban malaise has been ignored. Suburbia, by definition, is reactionary. The word means *sub*-urban—that is, *below* the city. Suburbs, middle-class and blue-collar alike, are created as reactions against the presumed, or real, evils of the city. They are reactionary in the sense that the persons populating them agree that the city—the principal unique and modern community form in our time—is not good and that a retreat to the rural is preferable.

Suburbia is psychologically and culturally as repressive as any big-city school committee or police force. The rigidly narrow zoning laws, the paranoiac exclusion of black people, the latent anti-Semitism, the uptight authoritarianism of school administrators, the upper middle-class preoccupation with college education, and the startling absence of political diversity—all are expressions of the reactionary and repressive nature of the suburban community. As suburbia is the seedbed for the middle-class mentality of the American social system at large, this repressiveness is a social problem of the first order. (For example, the House Un-American Activities Committee of the fifties was little more than a nit-picking coffee klatsch, writ dangerously large.)

What does this have to do with Christian education? Just this: As the reformulation of curricula in the sixties took into account the urban world, in the seventies it must deal with the suburban world. A special readjustment is needed. Suburban curricula cannot depend upon the disturbing, but rich, visual imagery of the urban world. Rather, it must contend with a cultural repressiveness which appears in compulsive behavior and visual blandness.

What is the answer? A *noncurriculum!* Repressive-compulsive behavior is not likely to be reoriented by a similarly compulsive and rigid educational medium. The inadequacy of this approach is being demonstrated in public education. The ladder-type of programmed education, where students progress rung by rung through a defined schedule of "knowledge," is a microcosm of the same students' year-by-year progress through the *right* nursery schools, the *right* grammar and high schools, and into the kingdom of the righteous—the college of one's choice. Tightly graded religious education material poses the same problem, only in a more subtle form.

Such rigidity must be confronted by a noncurriculum. A curriculum which isn't. A "study" guide that completely excises even the subtlest hint of ladder progressions, developmental chapters, and programmed knowledge.

The noncurriculum is experience-oriented, but with a radical departure from the former meaning of that term. Too often, in the past, experienced-based study programs have meant, "Let's make the church school classroom a laboratory of Christian love." And this, in turn, usually translated into a reluctance to expel disciplinary monsters from the fourth-grade boys' class because, "They must be taught that God loves all his children."

The noncurriculum is quite different. It refuses to require

the preexistence of any church or religious structure—not the church building, not the pious example of minister or deacon, not the church school class, and most certainly not a study outline in Christian thought and values.

The noncurriculum makes two presuppositions: (1) The world is created and sustained by God's power. (2) The world (and not the church) is the proper subject of Christian education. In other words, the noncurriculum takes seriously Colin Williams' now-famous imperative that the world write the agenda for the church.

My argument is that the noncurriculum has a special applicability to the suburban situation. Culturally, the suburbs suffer from an acute deprivation of experience of the larger world. Educationally, most suburban churches are encrusted with the narrowly exclusive and repressive mentality typical of any *intentional* ghetto. Only a drastic wrenching out of these repressive bonds and a daring plunge into the mysterious complexity of God's world can provide an education which, by its secular nature, becomes all the more Christian.

One church in a Boston suburb (Needham, Massachusetts) has experimented informally with noncurricula. In its adult education program, it has had one enormously successful program.

In the autumn of 1966, a group of women gathered for a six-week study program on the subject: Christian Ethics and World Problems. It soon became apparent to some group members that a discussion seminar on world problems was an absurd use of educational time. Instead, the group met with the Reverend Edward Blackman, director of the Commission on Housing for the United Church in Boston. Mr. Blackman quickly put this small group of inexperienced suburban women to work observing meetings of the Boston Housing Authority. They were greeted with instant hostility by the Authority, which was hypersensitive to outsiders meddling in official city business. The ladies, inexperienced in even so subtle a confrontation, backed off. Suddenly, some of their schedules got busy and they weren't sure they could make it. One member, for example, was concerned over possible trouble for her husband's business. The basic problem was lack of experience. With gentle persuasion and support, the group kept its original commitment.

In the end, their work produced very important results—both for the Commission on Housing and for themselves. Their observations and research contributed to the publication of a research report on the Boston Housing Authority. It was so effective that it played a major role in increasing Boston's awareness of its housing problem and in producing progressive shifts in the Authority itself.

For the women, the educational results were even more remarkable. They learned more about the urban world than any book could teach. By practical experience, they learned the skills of political research and confrontation. Most important, by the continuing necessity of justifying their actions to friends and neighbors and fellow church members back home, they became better theologians. It wasn't enough for them to meet the challenges of their less adventuresome suburban friends with platitudes. They were forced to develop a moral and theological rationale for their actions. At that point, theological and biblical material took on a new meaning.

One member of the group became so skilled at political analysis and group leadership that in the autumn of 1968 she was elected the first full-time executive director of the newly formed Needham Civil Rights Office—a position of responsibility totally unthinkable for her just two years before. Virtually every member of the group has discovered a new sense of responsibility for her church or community. All are involved now in similar projects in their hometown, bringing their newly acquired skills to bear on what for them is their primary responsibility: their own suburban town.

Noncurriculum is not merely a new form of the old suburban social-action ploy of tutoring "those poor ghetto kids" or throwing Christmas parties in settlement houses. The fundamental prerequisite of the noncurriculum must be effective participation in programs to confront, change, and reorganize the unjust structures of the world. The experience is painful and sometimes abrasive. It is difficult because not many are prepared for it. It is transforming because middle-class suburbanites are trained by culture to avoid the world's more serious problems. Such an involvement can shatter the reactionary impulses which reside in all our hearts.

15
YOUTH EMPOWERMENT

BY BOB BURT

The purpose of church education is simple. It is to make and keep life human, nothing more, nothing less. To fulfill that purpose, however, is not quite so simple. To do so demands a major shift in our educational focus to shouting alongside the victims of oppression, fighting for the establishment of justice, and affirming the reality and hope that man will prevail because God will prevail. And that does not mean a lot of talk by pious Sunday school teachers. It means some painful testing, some risk-taking, and some concrete actions by adults brave enough to join youth in the educational enterprise.

Now that may not be too easy for many. But for those few who might want to get on board, let's try to look at a few of our presuppositions which will have to change. To begin with, three new perspectives are necessary. The first is the establishment of an international perspective. It used to be fashionable for church school teachers to speak of one world, a sentimental affirmation of the unity of mankind. But such a world just does not exist. In reality there are three worlds. The developed West, the developed East, and the Third World of rising men and nations. It is the Third World to which we need to pay special attention and alongside which we need to build our educational programs and strategies. The Third World is made up of all those people who are the victims of the oppressive forces and the collective powers of West and East: the blacks in the United States, the young around the world, the peasants in Vietnam, Latin America, South Africa, Appalachia, and so on.

What makes them appear as one world is the vast network of communications which enables us to see, hear, and feel the pulsing cries of human beings thousands of miles away and even in our neglected backyards. Through the spectacles of the Third World, therefore, we develop a new international perspective, understanding that we live in a global village. Under these conditions, "Who is my neighbor?" is a newly pressing question. Answers to it involve foreign policy, economic development, political issues and structures, power realities—who has it? how is it changed? by what means?—and a host of other considerations usually untouched by church educators. It implies supporting youth in their challenges to our leadership and the structures of our systems. It means standing with them as they become a prophetic conscience in our culture. What I am trying to say is that as these considerations become the context for doing church education, both the context and the content change. The world—its character, its hopes, its meaning, its destiny—must become the context and the content for church education. In these times, church education is defined in concrete, behavioral terms: church education for peace, church education for economic justice, church education for full participation of blacks and the poor and the young in power distribution in a culture. The new content surfaces in the issues.

Why are the houses being torn down in order to expand the educational facilities without even consulting the former residents? Why do youth have no voice in the decision-making processes of their schools?

Why should young men participate in the systematic killing in a war they denounce?

Why should white youth accept student deferments when often their black brothers don't even have a choice?

If churches in this society are worth $85 billion, then why not give $500,000 in reparations to blacks who have been systematically kept out of white churches for centuries?

Second, the methodology of education must change. E. E. Cummings told his Harvard audience several years ago that he could not lecture to them because he didn't have anything to lecture about. All he could do was talk about himself. That's my point. No one has the answer. All we can do is talk about ourselves. Different peoples in different situations are experiencing different things. But if we do talk about ourselves and listen carefully to what others are telling us about their experiences, we can discern a sense of independence. People are taking the power to shape their own lives. Young people have a great many things to teach us.

Third, our style of education must change. Everywhere we look there is uncertainty and newness. It is important for church education and church educators to see these. Today the new is here but not yet shaped. As Columbia University student Mark Rudd put it, "I have no program. I have a dream of a better world than yours." These unsettled conditions plus the demands for changes can only precipitate conflict. Therefore, conflict must become a conscious and significant part of our educational style. This was beautifully illustrated in one congregation when a group of youth decided that the congregation should go on record favoring a unilateral withdrawal of American troops from Vietnam at its annual meeting. They lost. But in the months which followed, young people staged demonstrations outside and inside the sanctuary, before, after, and during sermons, engaged groups in discussion on the question, debated with the major boards and clergy. When the next congregational meeting came around, their position had enough support to pass. Their action was subsequently read into the *Congressional Record*, although no mention was made of how much conflict these people lived through in their maturing process.

These three new perspectives imply new ways of behaving. First, they mean an end to denominational church education. The formation of RISK in Rochester, New York, over the past couple years is illustrative of this point. In that city, since the great confrontation between FIGHT and the Eastman Kodak Company, demonstrational church education has ended as youth ministry programs have arisen in four different sectors of the city, each patterned after the peculiar nature of its section and composed of key congregations, leaders, and resources, Protestant and Catholic. They are: (1) Ecumenical Community Ministry, southwest sector, containing a high-density black population and a rapidly changing, integrating, white neighborhood; Immaculate Conception Parish, assuming the leadership role by hiring a minister specifically for the development of a center and a thrust into the problems and the police and courts and educational structures; (2) Area Youth Ministry, northwest sector, joining for the creation of a center and a program to face court and jail situations, as well as a group called the Committee Against White Racism to deal with the attitudes and structures of the community; (3) Southeast Area Youth Ministry, southeast sector, an economically, socially, racially heterogeneous area in transition including a great many poor white, black, and Puerto Rican families, several congregations having joined together for developing a strategy of research and action among the youth population in the area; (4) Northeast Area Youth Ministry, northeast sector, an increasingly black and Puerto Rican area with deteriorated housing and heavy industrial development. Ten congregations have united to create a center and to support youth congregations designed for community action and research into the structures of the area. In addition to these four sectors, similar suburban-based groups are being formed for strategic development both around these local issues and the total metropolitan ministry.

RISK is a movement toward concentrated training for leadership, determining church education priorities on a metropolitan scale, and planning for action in terms of institutional racism in the city.

Second, they mean new models of youth ministry. Let me tell you about the development of one. It began with a problem: Many youth are deeply concerned about our society, but they do not believe they can do anything to affect it. Powerlessness is a common feeling. Yet, the Christian is called to be a person of power. Enabling youth, therefore, to acquire the capacity and skills to act on behalf of just social change is an aim of church education. The question remains: How do you do it? One significant answer is found in the following model developed in a small Midwestern community by Episcopal and United Church of Christ congregations—some youth and adults, three local ministers, a state conference associate minister, a denominational youth staff member and a group of youth and adults from RISK, an interdenominational youth ministry funded by the Rochester, New York, diocese of the Roman Catholic Church.

The event was a conference involving ten youth, six adults, and the gang from RISK—twenty-two in all. It went something like this: Friday, the group gathered and immediately began to identify those issues which they thought the church needed to address. An attempt was made to break the issues down into categories. The list looked like this:

Government—selective service, the Vietnam War, imperialism, nationalism, military-industrial complex, patriotism, amnesty.

Black—persecution of the Panthers, racism, black revolution, American Indian.

Law—drugs, abortion, selective service, capital punishment, censorship, welfare, pollution, population control, court system.

Religion—relevancy of the church, celebration.

Poverty—grape strike, migrant workers.

Education—curriculum, student power, innovation.

By the end of the morning session, education was voted as their priority issue. During the afternoon, they divided into three groups to develop action proposals on education. That evening the proposals were read.

The first local group made their statement:

We decided that we needed revamping of the teaching methods and a more innovative school system. This can be done by relating to the students with new media such as role playing, etc. Also a breakdown of the authoritarian teacher/student relationship is needed. One suggestion for implementing change is that students simply suggest their ideas to teachers. One system to modify grades is seek student support. Then either petition administration or have the student government ratify our proposal.

The second local group's report read:

We believe that the current educational system is inadequate and artificial and that it stifles creativity. We therefore need wider experimentation and opportunities for freedom of thought. We propose that one method for accomplishing this would be the establishment of a free school, i.e. special courses not allied with any current system offered by qualified resource people and others interested.

An intellectual discussion followed. Then it happened. The RISK group read their proposal:

We are surrounded by systems that are both oppressive and dehumanizing, and one that has a great effect on our lives is the educational system. Thus, we need to deal with it directly. Your experience in the community of attempting to act within the system and our experience in Rochester along the same lines is met with continual frustration and no significant change. Thus, we have decided that change from within is no longer a viable alternative. Therefore, we propose that this conference of students take the following positive expression toward liberation.

On Monday, December 1, the beginning of Advent, we should demonstrate our celebration of hope by disrupting the administrative functions of the high school. Part of this disruption shall be a confiscation of the personal history files in the school which in reality decide what our personal future is going to be. These files are a source of great psychological and economic oppression, psychological in that they submit the individual's future style of life to the decisions of an elitist corps. In many cases, these judgments have been biased. Economic oppression is evidenced when history files prohibit people from gaining employment that is personally fulfilling. This act shall be our statement of resistance to an oppressive and dehumanizing system.

Now everyone was involved. There was little agreement over the tactics. Here was a specific proposal for action. Few had experience in dealing with statements calling for specific commitment and action.

The confrontation between the two groups grew in intensity. The RISK group defended their proposal as the only viable way for change to take place. Individuals went off by themselves to think. Small groups gathered to talk. Attempts were made to write other proposals. The adults struggled to be silent, to listen and stay on the edge, to hear what the young people themselves would do. That evening was particularly trying for one of the ministers, the father of two of the participants. His young people were finding it difficult to say what they thought, what they really thought, until finally at midnight in the silence of the room a sophomore stood up very haltingly and said: "I do not like and I cannot support this proposal. I know what my parents would think about it and I think they're right. I could not do this to my mother."

At that moment, that young man became a man. He took a position. He acted. With his words, the group decided to go to bed. A decision would have to wait until morning.

Saturday morning, when they gathered, the RISK group suggested that instead of reconsidering the proposals they begin to look at some other educational symbols such as report cards, demerit systems, trophies, flag poles, letter sweaters, black students, and libraries. Books became the immediate focal point of the group's concern. All the books in the school library reflect one point of view. That had to be changed. They talked about churches giving money to buy books representing positions other than those already found in their school library. They considered presenting the new books to the library and they thought about taking out as many books as possible from the school library and keeping them until the library added books of more diverse opinions.

A small group from the community and some of the RISK youth became a committee to formulate a new proposal. When they regathered, the new proposal was adopted.

In the afternoon, they broke up into task groups to decide what books they would buy, how they would confront local churches with the issue, how they would get the money to purchase the books, and how they would handle the presentation of the books to the school. For the first time, there was commitment and excitement. They had become a concerned community. There was even time now for a little football, fun, and laughter. They had made a decision and they were on their way toward action.

Some of the books bought during the afternoon were: *Institutional Racism in America*, edited by Lewis L. Knowles and Kenneth Brewitt; *The Vietnam Hearings*, edited by J. William Fulbright; *How to Stay Out of the Army*, edited by Conrad Lynn; *Five Plays* by Langston Hughes; *The Shame of the Cities*, Lincoln Steffens; *Post-Prison Writings and Speeches*, Eldridge Cleaver; *The Right of Revolution*, Truman Nelson; *Death at an Early Age*, Jonathan Kozol; *Summerhill*, A. S. Neill; *Ho Chi Minh, a Political Biography*, Jean Lacouture; *36 Children*, Herbert Kohl; *The Last Year of Malcolm X*, George Breitman; *The Black Panthers*, Gene Marine; and *Reminiscences of the Cuban Revolutionary War*, Che Guevara.

Saturday evening they gathered again. The youth were ready to put a question to the adults: Where are you? How much support can you give? How do you feel about us confronting your congregation on Sunday with the issue? Are you willing to face a hostile congregational response to the books we want in school?

The immediate adult response was weak. They weren't sure that they liked everything about the idea. As one minister put it, "We gave very thin support." Their reaction pushed the youth further against the wall. They didn't have the support they had expected and hoped for. Their position was being seriously questioned. Then one young man stood up in frustration and said, "It's clear that we cannot bring ourselves to any meeting of the minds. We don't know where we are. I've had enough. I'm packing and leaving." In silence, he rolled up his sleeping bag, packed his duffle and walked out. That took courage. Yet what made it a dramatic moment was the fact that he was the son of one of the ministers present.

One of the adults from RISK spoke:

I don't know if you young people have really seen what has happened here. It took courage for a young man to express in word and deed his convictions, including his opposition to his own father, and it took courage for a father to let it happen.

In the silence that followed, everyone changed. The minister later wrote,

At that moment, I ceased to be the pastor of a congregation, responsible for an institution, fearful for it. I found myself a father, completely overwhelmed with a sense that I had let my son down, perhaps that I had also let a lot of other sons and daughters down. And I wept because I couldn't help it. Your children and mine saw the dignified, aloof, removed minister weep and I had to leave.

There were tears in the group, choked voices, and then a decision. The library proposal would be acted upon.

They would confront the churches with the issue and a request for money on Sunday morning. The ministers would give them free time to make their proposal to the congregation. By now the RISK group was unimportant. They were pushed into the background. They weren't needed anymore. They had fulfilled their role as witness and catalyst to a process and a way of life. The youth from this small community had learned from them what it was to be powerful.

They developed a statement to be presented in the churches on Sunday morning.

We, a group of high school students, are concerned with the quality of education we are receiving and want to do something to correct the situation. One of the very weaknesses lies in our school library which fails to provide books representing a wide range of opinion, political thought, and human experience. We are asking your aid to solve the problem. We, a church conference of high school students, feel that the high school library must give a more complete picture of the contemporary world. Therefore, we request you donate money to augment the library with books that present ideas other than those just expressed in the classroom.

The statement was mimeographed and handed out to people as they arrived at church. The youth defended their position during the service. After the service, the youth discussed their concern with the parishioners. Money was collected. But it wasn't all that simple. A good deal of disagreement and opposition to their cause was expressed. They were learning what it was like to be fought against. They discovered that making decisions and acting was complex and caused reactions that could not always be anticipated.

That evening, they gathered to work further on their strategy. News releases were written and leaflets were mimeographed to be passed out to the student body. They wanted everyone to understand what they were doing and why. They made a decision to give the books to the principal instead of the librarian. They prepared a statement to go with the books, which read:

We, a group of high school youth, present fifty books to the library of our school with the hope of making a positive step toward the improvement of our school. These books are for all students and symbolize our active desire for bettering our school. We feel that this action is completely constructive because it provides a wider list of reading materials for all students. We have raised money by going to our churches. Today, we present the books to you for our library.

The principal had been expecting them; he had already received many phone calls from citizens about the event at the churches. Pressure from teachers and parents began to be put on him. He told them he would have to refer the issue to the superintendent. The superintendent, they discovered, wouldn't handle it. He referred the issue to the school board. This procedure attempted to avoid a decision when everyone knew that the principal could have simply accepted the books. But he was unwilling to make a decision. The group of youth did not give up. They had learned what it was to have the capacity to act for a democratic social change. They were not going to stop until the books were on the shelves, no matter what the opposition. Happily, we can report that most of the books have made their way to the school shelves. A few are still in question. The youth are still pressing to have their action completed. They have learned how their school operates and where decisions are made. They know how difficult it is to effect change but also how, with the right strategy, change can be effected. They learned what it is to be a person in power, to have the capacity to act, to deal with issues and in the light of their Christian faith make decisions. The RISK people have left. Those who remain will never be the same. They have learned something very important. No classroom could teach what that educational experience taught.

They know now what it is to dramatize an issue, to involve their churches, to effect action, and to change the system. Hopefully, they will not become disillusioned and, like some youth, turn to anarchy as the only way out of an unjust system. Hopefully, they will have learned what it is to effect change and that they can be agents of change. The adults learned, too.

It became clear that learning doesn't come from having information pushed into our heads but from living through experiences and trying to reflect upon them. They discovered that a good conference only needs a place to meet, some food, and a group of people with a purpose. They had no schedules, no planned recreation, no program. But they did have a job to do. No one could remember anyone saying he was bored. They discovered that structure takes care of itself when there is something worth doing. The conference was held in a church in the midst of many distracting influences. But it was this factor which made the conference significant. In these circumstances, they had to face the consequences of their actions. (It's always easier when you're away from home to be radical and idealistic. When you're at home and being asked to act on your words, it's a different situation.) The fact that the group was able to take a significant piece of action amidst all the pressures of being at home was no small accomplishment. They learned what it was to make responsible decisions and to be responsible for their actions. This attempt at educational innovation has been evaluated a success. Refinements still need to be made and new exploration into aspects of this educational model developed. One thing has become clear. This kind of educational model will be important in the future of education with youth in the church.

THE FAMILY ALTERNATIVE

BY J. THOMAS LEAMON

"We've given up on the church school." Jim, a young father, was explaining his family's alternative to parish-oriented Christian education. He spoke with a trace of sadness, perhaps guilt; he was a deacon of his church. "But it seemed to us that the whole church school procedure was saying to our children, 'Check your minds at the door.' "

"Yeah," added Becky, a bright third-grader. "They never let you ask any good questions." Becky was helping her sister, Ann, assemble the materials for the family's Sunday morning teach-in. Ten-year-old Ann knew her job: an overflowing box of crayons, a sheaf of paper, chairs for everyone at the dining-room table including a high-chair for kindergarten Johnny—and a final reminder to her father to bring the Bible.

Jim gave the morning's scriptures a last-minute look. Then the family was seated and Jim started reading the first chapter of Ezekiel. "In the thirtieth year, in the fourth month, . . . as I was among the exiles by the river Chebar, the heavens were opened, and I saw visions of God. . . . As I looked, behold, a stormy wind came out of the north, and a great cloud, . . . and fire flashing forth continually. . . ." The voice was careful, precise, even pedantic, clearly respectful, stumbling over a word now and again, not always connecting with the meaning.

His wife's brow furrowed as the great surrealistic vision progressed. "What do you suppose Ezekiel had in mind when he talks about creatures with four faces—the face of an ox, a lion, an eagle, and a man? Was he using symbolism? Did he have a hidden meaning?" Sylvia wondered in her best analytic academic manner. Becky gave her mother a delighted grin. As the esoteric details of Ezekiel's vision emerged, Becky stretched her arms above her head, making spontaneous dancing gestures: "And the living creatures darted to and fro, like a flash of lightning. . . . Over the heads of the living creatures there was the likeness of a firmament, shining like crystal. . . . And when they went, I heard the sound of their wings like the sound of many waters, like the thunder of the Almighty. . . ."

"You know why he says all those things, Mom?" Becky asked. "It's so you'll know that God is (and here she gave an imitation of a trumpet fanfare) ta-ta-ta-taaaaaa!! You know, like in the song, 'And dark is his path on the wings of the storm.' "

Becky, with a child's certain receptivity of feeling, immediately caught the sense, the import, the mood of Ezekiel's vision. She had not gotten hung up on a labored literal symbolism of each of the images but had gone to the heart of the matter. Ezekiel was trying to convey a sense of the grandeur and the majesty of God. And the vivid jumble of images made her feel like dancing an accompaniment.

The reading progressed. The group around the table interrupted freely with questions, discussion, comments. As a visitor in the circle, I spoke somewhat diffidently of how Ezekiel was using everything out of his world, everything he could think of—animals, minerals, manufactured things like chariots, weather, and human images—to describe something of what God is like. We wondered: How would people today describe God? What *is* God like?

Just before the talk might have started to sag, Jim asked Ann to say the prayer that morning. Ann prayed directly and openly about events and problems of the week, naturally bringing in the discussion of Ezekiel. Then Jim reached for his guitar and the family sang a song they'd known before, "Ezekiel Saw the Wheel"—the spiritual—and, recognizing Becky's insight, sang two verses of "O Worship the King." The final happening was a distribution of crayons and paper for a visual interpretation of Ezekiel's vision, with everyone describing his picture and asking questions about the others. Even five-year-old John had a delightful contribution to the family encounter with Ezekiel. It looked rather like a flight of Boeing 747s, each with four fuzzy heads.

"We've been doing this about two years," Sylvia said over her shoulder as she peeled potatoes for the noon meal. "It started when we were especially disenchanted with a Christmas service. It was inane and thoughtless, and everyone was bored. So we went home and wrote our own Advent service. It came out so well that then and there we decided to have our own church school." She said that neither she nor her husband was eager to subvert or weaken the regular church school. "Neither of us wants to start an underground church," she said. "If other parents are satisfied with what goes on in the church school, that's perfectly okay with us. Jim and I aren't willing to teach in the church school, so we don't feel that we have any right to make a fuss about what's going on. The reason we don't teach is that teaching makes such a hassle of Sunday morning. We feel that Sunday is the only day our family gets to see each other, and we're not willing to go rushing off in five separate directions this day, too."

The parents spoke of their great enjoyment in the Saturday night planning. "We've so enjoyed hashing it over between us," said Sylvia. "Jim and I have talked about things like: What is life after death? And: Who is God? I can deal more effectively with Jesus than I can with God," she added, perhaps thinking of her encounter with Becky and Ezekiel. Jim explained, "I wanted to be able to say something to the kids besides 'Hrrumph' and a quick look aside," he said. "I want to be able to look them in the eye and say frankly, 'I haven't made up my mind about that yet.' Or, 'I don't know, but I'm thinking about it.'"

Few families, I'm sure, are willing to follow the discipline this family follows. Jim and Sylvia buy, read, and discuss books on theology, ethics, and the Bible. They have read much of Bonhoeffer. They read biblical commentaries. It is important to them that their children be familiar with the content of the Bible, that the kids have a clear sense of the family's religious values and identity. Yet they want the biblical knowledge to be related to experience and the sense of identity to be more than formal tokenism. One or two other families drop in for church school occasionally, but they know of no other families in their college-town church who feel as they do or who follow a similar routine.

I was touched and moved to be a part of this experience. It was delightful to observe the contribution a child's openness to feeling can make to adult intellectualism. It was a joy to observe a family where a child felt free to feel. I was inspired to discover a family genuinely and creatively concerned about religious education and religious traditions in an intelligent yet unassuming way. The family's energy and initiative and creativity are wholly admirable. Setting the Bible in its cultural spectrum—relating folk song and hymnody and, sometimes, the visual arts to scripture—is valuable.

As a pastor, I did worry about the family's relationship to the church. I know they face hard alternatives: they shouldn't be expected to become tame Christians, making themselves dutifully subservient to a congregation and a clergyman dull and dreadfully routine. Nor should they be spurred into becoming the butt of undercover resentments and anger that are the lot of too many reformers in too many parishes. But an important part of the sense of the church is the relationship, the ministries, among a people, and this feature is lacking in the privatism of a single family.

I worry, too, about what I'll call the "privatism" of the family curriculum, for want of a better word. It's no better or worse than the privatism of any pastor's preaching schedule, I suppose, but the selections of scripture a family chooses could become quite narrow and limited by the family's limitations of training or knowledge. This family had been picking brief events from the life of Jesus or from the Bible—parables, sayings, and so on. One picture on the family bulletin board illustrated Ann's concept of the "widow's mite." Another vivid expressionist work was Johnny's visualization of Jesus about to be thrown off a cliff by neighbors convinced that a prophet has no honor in his own country.

Adaptability, or an openness to curriculum being suggested by the needs or life of the group, is an asset in this format, as it is in any other educational setting. One weekend, when the parents were planning to read some psalms as a reflection of the lovely autumn environment, five-year-old John came into the kitchen as lunch was being prepared. "Mom," he said, "is your head the most important part of your body?" Out went the psalms, in came Paul's passage on the body of Christ from 1 Corinthians 12. (John was delighted that his question gave rise to Sunday's class!)

The interpretive drawings were memorable. Ann drew a person who was mostly nose. Becky drew a person who was all head, with minute arms and legs. Jim drew a being who was all foot. "They're monsters!" the children laughed. And the family came to the conclusion that anyone who overemphasizes one function or one piece of anatomy, who isn't in some kind of proportion or balance, is a monster. The discussion turned to ecology and to keeping the balance of nature. Man becomes monstrous when he overemphasizes production and profit. Interestingly, the genitals were never mentioned in the enumeration of important body parts, thus proving the family to be faithfully Pauline, though not necessarily, in this regard, to their benefit.

An unexpected dividend was the children's appreciation of Paul as a person. As the children drew the implications of Paul's written images of disproportionate man, and as they laughed at the resulting grotesques, they commented on what a sense of humor and wit Paul must have had. "This was one of our best sessions," reports Sylvia. "Other times, we fall flat."

Perhaps a church might encourage its families to engage in education after this pattern, on a parish-wide basis. And perhaps the pastor and education committee could prepare a well-considered variety of passages for study and family discussion, with groups of parents coming for week-night preparation. Resources of music and art could be supplied by the church, out of a frame of reference sometimes wider and deeper than that of an individual family. There could be periodic informal sharing sessions where the values of a church's wider fellowship could be preserved.

"Perhaps"—"could"—"should" it's all pretty theoretical, anyhow. I really don't believe there are many Protestants interested enough in the Bible or in religious tradition to go through such a routine as I've described, let alone to make it such a rewarding part of their family routine. But for me, for an hour, it was a beautiful alternative.

17
LEARNING CLUSTERS

BY EDNA STUMPF

I think, sometimes, that learning takes us backward rather than forward. The longer we gaze at the phenomenon of human development, the more we realize that we are simply looking at ourselves and the personal histories that formed us. And there is no single factor more important to a person's history than his family. Not yet, anyway.

I was not thinking things like this on the plane to Rochester, New York, last April, but I have been thinking them since. In Rochester there is a large, suburban church—quite prosperous-looking, with about twenty-five bulletin boards and almost that many doors—and what was bruited to be a highly unusual system of religious education. We had heard about that system at *Colloquy*. It was called "family clusters." It was still, like everything else worth mentioning in education, in the experimental stages.

The innovator of this model of family clusters is Margaret Sawin, "teaching minister" of First Baptist Church. Dr. Sawin is soft-spoken, white-haired, ladylike—all of which tends to work in your favor if you're engaged in an experiment. She treated me to an extremely good dinner not long after my plane landed, and we discussed families. I mentioned that the nuclear family was having its problems—not going so far as to suggest, as others have, that it may be on its way out. Dr. Sawin agreed about the problems, and she didn't mention that it may be on its way out either. I don't think either one of us believed that it was, to tell the truth. The family is probably going to hang around for the millennium, just for spite.

But the tensions of the family are real, although the polite atmosphere of the congregation seems to suffocate them as much as do the clichés of the last years: incompatibility, juvenile delinquency, the generation gap. Parents are often unhappy with each other and their children; children are often unhappy with each other and their parents. One might quote Milos Forman, Czechoslovakian refugee and film director: "I discovered a lot of love and no understanding. Taken individually, each member of the family would be kind, but when they all got together, they only seemed interested in hurting each other." The family may be falling apart. The thing is that its members, in some cases and for some periods of time, are still all to be found in the same pew.

Which is why, pointed out Dr. Sawin, the church should do something to provide first-aid for families. "If someone had inquired some years ago whether this church did something for families, the answer would have been: 'Of course—we preach nice sermons, we have a graded Sunday School . . .' " But the church can do more than that. It has an opportunity. "The church is the only institution in society that includes all generations."

Thus: "family clusters," four or five families gathering weekly in an open-ended kind of experience. Eating together, playing games, staging skits, holding discussions, answering questions. Sometimes just sitting around and talking or—a trickier endeavor—being quiet together.

Although there are "units" (ten to twelve weeks) and "objectives" (family history, poverty, values, and beliefs) the approach in family clusters is unpressured and the learning aids —games, reading matter—are chosen with care from week to week. The content is there, but it's the communication that matters.

There are three family clusters at First Baptist, each different in terms of makeup, duration, group sensibility, problems. There are children in all of them, single women in at least two. In each cluster, members have committed themselves to meeting each other every week—a commitment which seems to become more complex and formidable the longer it lasts. The cluster is not so much a cluster of people as it is a cluster of relationships. "A possibility of 236 first-time interactions going on during a two-hour period!" writes Dr. Sawin impressively, not forgetting the exclamation point. And then she provides a loaded footnote. "An interaction is any way two persons have of communicating with each other, either verbally or nonverbally. This is the 'heart' of the growth process and the ability to share with one another."

So much for what families and education and the Christian church have to do with each other: the "interaction" is at the center of all three. Learning how to understand (appreciate, love) and live (communicate) with each other are worthy goals for family education and worthy goals for Christian education. The learning involved is a tentative and gradually strengthening awareness of the presence of others. A dispensing with useless defenses and dishonesties. The humble risk that some people have always taken, in the name of this faith, in being together.

This is not an easy thing. Hidden in the most open group of human beings—family members—is the inevitable anxiety that our way of life has trained us to feel when we reveal ourselves to others without benefit of a program. Parents "watch" their children—restrain them, on occasion. They object, by way of the brief questionnaires which the cluster leaders send out on occasion like feelers, to too much "sensitivity" material. Adolescents sometimes pull away, resisting togetherness in the time-honored way of adolescents. But the meetings continue, and the interactions go on.

There is no typical cluster meeting. I attended two and they were quite different. Dr. Sawin acts as co-leader of two clusters, sharing the role of guide-observer with students of Colgate Divinity School, Ann Petter and David Harwood. Two other persons do the planning for the third group: Ann Powell, parishioner, and student David Tompkinson. The Anns and Davids are young, busy, and idealistic in the matter-of-fact way of people who know they are onto something new and demonstrably growing. The things to be discovered are limitless; the challenge for new leadership could swamp the movement. The students hold meetings with co-leaders, general meetings, meetings with Dr. Sawin and Dr. Edward Thornton of Colgate-Rochester Divinity School, Department of Pastoral Care. They make classes and raise families and keep smiling and keep moving. They like what they're doing, and they have to.

Guiding a cluster gives new life to the dead phrase "working with people." The method is to try something, to watch the results with the eye of a hawk, to decide on the next step. The first night of my visit, a little girl who had called herself "the most unimportant member of Cluster" brought in a game for everyone to play. There were two handicapped persons in the group, and they were able to participate. The game turned out well. We all had a real good time. I personally carried away considerable respect for that little girl's status. Following the game was a collection of miniskits, meant to describe good and bad moments in the life of each family. They weren't high in dramatic value but they were revealing—more revealing than I had suspected before sitting in on the post-cluster analysis. In such indirect ways can the leaders sense what "families" don't usually tell outsiders: who dominates, who resists, who suffers, who hopes for and needs security or change. The

LEARNING CLUSTERS

next evening two leaders challenged another group to build "family sculptures" from cloth, clothes hangers, fake flowers —in silence. The results looked fine to me, if opaque in terms of meaning. I can't imagine what directions those small pieces of combined imagination suggested to Ann Powell and Dave Tompkinson.

Cluster leaders tread a fine line. Sensitized and trained as they are, even pressured as students to produce "project" results, they could be tempted to see these family groups as laboratories complete with two generations of guinea pigs. But I didn't catch that. The atmosphere of the cluster meeting is warm, fairly conventional, with overtones of "Christian fellowship" going back more than a century. The kids won't always sit still and, fortunately, policy states that they don't have to. The adults know each other pretty well and can relax; they've been sharing meals for months. Members embark on the challenges of the evening with little resistance and much enthusiasm, although they know that they are being watched and can't, in all honesty, show themselves in their best light. At any moment a worry, an emotion, is going to burst out—only to return the next week in the form of a game, a discussion, a private question to answer in the corner, perhaps with block capitals and a shaky pencil. The curriculum is awareness, and everyone contributes.

This is why Margaret Sawin cannot imagine a "standard curriculum" for family clusters. There is no way to standardize the individual, multiplied as he is in his hundreds of relationships and determined as he is not to be readily understood, even by himself. In this sense, the unstructured "education for living" that is the whole point of family clusters bears a weird resemblance to the open-classroom method of elementary education, to which I have paid particular attention recently. There are a thousand ways to help a human being learn, apparently, but if you want to eliminate bad side effects, there is no single way to force him to learn. His pace is his own.

Family Clusters have been around, in Rochester, slightly more than two years. They are spreading—in Rochester, and elsewhere. New leaders are being trained. Feedback is turning into usable research. Dr. Sawin is hopefully planning a book on developing family clusters. "The time is right." That may just wrap it up. The time just may be right for people everywhere in their separated roles and homes and age classifications to start being with and learning from each other. Would retribalization be too strong a word? Margaret Sawin sensibly states that she is not dealing with communes, where "living-in" is the indispensable requirement. A family cluster does not create something entirely new, but it strives to recreate something eternal: openness and trust between individuals.

Of course, it is out of such trust that new things always come.

18
VALUE EDUCATION

BY SIDNEY B. SIMON

THREE WAYS TO TEACH CHURCH SCHOOL

So much teaching, even colorful, dynamic and flamboyant teaching, never gets beyond the "fact" level. I remember a college physics professor who stunned his audience one day. In a crowded, tiered lecture hall he suspended a giant steel ball on a thin cable. He dragged the ball up to the top row, held it against his nose with the cable taut, and let it go. Then he stood there, waiting, while the ball reached the end of its arc and headed back toward his nose. The class gasped as the ball approached closer and closer, ready to knock him over. Of course, the law of physics prevailed and the ball stopped just short of clobbering him in the head. The class learned a fact: A pendulum loses inertia with each swing. That fact would appear on a true and false question on the midterm exam. It was an important but isolated fact and in a sense a "so what?" fact. Despite the sheer drama of his teaching, this professor was still operating on the fact level, the lowest of the three levels of teaching.

The second and higher level is the "concept level." Here, a series of facts is linked and generalizations drawn from them. At the concept level, there are fewer multiple-choice and short-answer tests. A teacher is more likely to use essay questions to evaluate the learning. This is obviously more complex teaching and more exciting learning. As a parent, I would be quite happy if all of my children's teachers moved beyond the fact level and taught at the concept level. (The millennium, however, is many light-years away. Another law of inertia and one my physics instructor didn't understand.)

Concept-level teaching is very good teaching, but there is still a more desirable kind of teaching at a third level. It may be the most important level of all. It is what I call values-level teaching. It directly involves a student in examining his own values. It asks many "you" questions and insists that the student confront issues suggested by the content. These issues should involve him in choices which are relevant to his day-to-day life.

Can this third level of teaching be done with the typical content of a typical church school course? I would answer with a resounding *yes*. Not only can it be done, it must be done if we are to make of church school more than a once-a-week platter of platitudes.

TWO EXAMPLES
The Triumphant Entry into Jerusalem
(Mark 11:1-19 and Luke 19:28-40)

I. Fact Level:
    What instructions did Jesus give his two disciples?
    Did it go just as Jesus said it would go?
    What was the reaction of the Pharisees to the large
        crowd of Jesus' disciples who were praising him?
    How did Jesus answer the Pharisees?

II. Concept Level:
    What is the meaning of Jesus riding into the city of Jerusalem on an ass?

What were the people who threw palm branches before
him expecting to have happen?
What are the important distinctions between the Phari-
sees and the disciples?

III. Values Level:
Would you have been able to turn over the tables of
money-changers in the temple? Wasn't this violent
and destructive of private property? Is this anything
like the cases of students who force deans out of
their offices? Or like the cases of persons who burn
draft board files? Have you ever participated in an act
that destroyed property? Name a time when you feel
you could do so. The disciples seemed to have no
embarrassment about demonstrating their beliefs in
public. How easy is it for you to announce to anyone
what you believe when it is unpopular or you might be
punished for doing so? Have you ever participated in
a demonstration for civil rights or to end the war in Vietnam? Why? What kind of demonstrations do you
think are acceptable? When should people participate in a demonstration?

These values questions are merely suggestive. Other
teachers might be interested in using the story to get at a
whole different range of values questions. Important, however, is the idea that the third level of teaching always focuses
on the "you" and is relevant to the student's life. There should
not be any effort made to have every student come out with a
single set of "right" values. Values are very complex and very
personal; there are no "right" values.

St. Francis of Assisi
I. Fact Level:
What was St. Francis' real name? Where and when was
he born?

What were the events which led up to his turning over
  his old life?

What were his father's reactions?

What kind of clothes did St. Francis wear? What did they
  represent?

How did Pope Innocent III react to all of this?

What were the "stigmata" St. Francis acquired?

Why is he almost always pictured with birds nearby?

Did he die from leprosy?

II.   Concept Level:

How far apart were the lives of the poor and the rich in
  the early thirteenth century when St. Francis lived? St.
  Francis claimed that he was married to "Lady Poverty." Why was this such an unorthodox statement for
  a man of God to make at that time? What else was
  unorthodox about St. Francis?

Pope Innocent had a real dilemma in dealing with St.
  Francis. What were the issues surrounding the
  pope's problem?

How do you explain the rapid spread of the Friars?

St. Francis literally worked himself to death, and even
  upon dying he thanked his Lord. Can you explain
  that?

What was St. Francis' contribution to the church and
  why does he earn a place in its history?

III. Values Level:

How near do the poor live to you? How much concern
  should you have about their poverty? Have you ever
  done anything about it? Can anything be done? By
  you? If not you, by whom?

Do you know your own father well enough to know his
  reaction if you were to do what St. Francis did? Explain.

St. Francis was able to get through to the pope. What

would you try to get the pope to accept if you were able to reach him? Would your writing a letter do any good? Explain.

Many men today also work themselves to death. Many others have ulcers, or smoke or drink too much because of their work. What does that say to you about your own life? What are you going to do about it?

Almost any subject matter can be viewed at the three levels discussed in this article. If we examine the teaching in our church schools, I am afraid we will find entirely too much on the first level. Facts are important. You can't build concepts without them. You can't make values choices without first examining as many alternatives as possible, and alternatives grow out of facts. What is needed, though, is more effort to go beyond the fact level. And beyond the concept level. We need more content to confront students where they live. As we do, we turn church schools into something much more viable and relevant. It could also help us teachers to clarify our own values. Not bad, for a Sunday morning. Even sleeping late couldn't feel as good.

YOUR VALUES ARE SHOWING

The following is a series of value clarity exercises that can be used by teachers and students—and families and friends—to help individuals discover and articulate their values.

VALUES SHEETS

Values sheets consist of a provocative, controversial statement, usually by a contemporary writer. After the statement, the teacher poses four to six questions. These are designed to make the students think about where they stand on the topic. Sheets should be mimeographed so that each student has his own copy.

The class is given time to think and write out its answers.

Later, a discussion will flow naturally; the design of the values sheet prohibits neutrality. As always, the teacher enters the discussion, accepting viewpoints different from his own. The following are some values sheets used by teachers in the past:

"Under the Sway of the Great Apes"

Edwin P. Young, an uncelebrated philosopher, once observed of football, "After all, it's only a game that kids can play." This is no longer strictly true. If it were, the networks would not have bought it up as a vehicle to sell cigarettes, cars and beer.

The evidence suggests that it satisfies some inner need of the spectator so completely that it can rivet him to his chair through a holiday in disregard of family life or bring him to his feet howling for (Allie) Sherman's head when the outcome fails to gratify.

If sports have ceased to be only games that kids can play and become psychotherapy for the mob, it is too bad, especially for kids who will grow up hating them or busting gussets to achieve therapeutic professional excellence.

What is worse, though, is the distortion of values that radiates throughout the society. For thirty minutes of farce, Liston and Clay can earn more than the entire faculty of a public school can make in a decade.[1]

1) Did you watch football on New Year's Day?

2) Is it a pattern of yours? Is it something about which you are proud?

3) How would you answer Mr. Baker?

4) Do you think the publishers of *Harpers* or *Atlantic* could benefit from taking ads during the televising of a football game? Comment.

5) Does this sheet make you want to do anything different in your life?[2]

Excerpt from *The Harvesters*

Asked where he secured his seasonal workers, the personnel director of an industrial farm on the eastern seaboard said:

"I tell you, I've been in this business for twenty-eight years. Back in the thirties we used day hauls from the cities; you know, Italians and Polocks and Hunkies and people like that. In the early forties we had prisoners of war, and sometimes we've contracted for British West Indians. These past years we've had Negro families from the South and some Puerto Ricans, sugar-cane workers off the Island. They change as the years go by, but I'll tell you one thing for sure. When spring comes, whoever they are, they're the people who are the hungriest. Who else wants to work that hard for that little money?" [3]

1. List the fruits and vegetables you and your family ate yesterday. Can you speculate on the human beings who were involved in getting them to your table?

2. Would it help if you just quit eating celery? What would help more?

3. Answer the man who says this: "I have no prejudice because they are migrants, nor even because they are Negroes. I simply believe that we need to take a long-range view of this problem. If we place too much emphasis on getting them into school, they will grow up unwilling to do stoop labor. Then where will our country be?"

4. What do you think you would learn by being a migrant worker for one week? Is it worth learning? Explain.

"I Have No Time"

I have no time for world peace groups;
    I am a mother
My days are spent with cod-liver oil
    and baths in the sun—

So my son's sturdy limbs will better adorn
A barbed barricade
Somewhere afar, years to come, slain
By a lad like himself.

I have no time to write Congressmen
   Urging neutrality,
Indeed no! I am too busy cooking
   Dried prunes—
So the blood from his young chest
Will redder and redder run
When he drops lifeless in some foreign land
Protecting investments.

I have no time to study why wars are:
I am raising a son,
Cleaning, polishing, ironing white rompers—
Then, hypnotized by fife and drum,
Stabbing with madness,
Ripping out hearts with a bright bayonet
He will slaughter his brothers.
I have no time.

by Margaret T. Gibbs—1938

1. What are some of the things you would tell this woman if you met her?

2. In what ways are you like she is?

3. If World War III comes tomorrow, what part will you have had in allowing it to happen?

4. What can we do together to put an end to war?

5. What will you personally be willing to do?

WEEKLY VALUES CARDS

After a six-week run on reaction sheets, a teacher might try using values cards. A values card is simply a 4 × 6 card upon which is written something a student cares about deeply. This can be written in any length, style, or form. No topic is forbidden. They are not to be graded or even corrected for spelling or grammar.

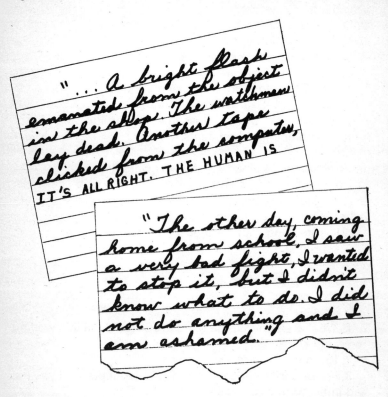

"... A bright flash emanated from the object in the shop. The watchman lay dead. Another tape clicked from the computer, IT'S ALL RIGHT, THE HUMAN IS

"The other day, coming home from school, I saw a very bad fight, I wanted to stop it, but I didn't know what to do. I did not do anything and I am ashamed."

Students sign their names on their cards. They may, however, write on them: "Please do not read to class." The cards which do not have that stipulation are read occasionally out loud to the class, anonymously. The unidentified author usually joins the lively discussion which follows.

Values cards open students up to new ideas. Students are confronted with their peers' thinking.

From time to time, the teacher should return the cards, asking questions regarding any patterns he sees. This kind of evaluation advances the clarification process. One thing is clear to any teacher who has read a stack of values cards each week for a year: they certainly beat the material students grind out for English compositions. One of the differences: values are personal and relevant.

VALUES CONTINUUM

A continuum is used to break down either/or thinking. It takes a problem which usually splits people into two oversimplified camps and opens it up to show a wide range of intellectually defensible positions.

Take the draft. It is not enough to say someone is a dove or a hawk. There are many complex reasons why one person's values lead him to enlist at the earliest possible date and why another would rather go to prison than serve in the army.

Set up preposterous positions at either end of the continuum. The hope is that these positions will be so far out that no one would dare support them. Take this continuum: at one extreme is Eager Egbert. He is so committed to the military that he has been trying to enlist since he was eleven. Now he is fourteen and he is trying for the ninetieth time to look older so he can go to Vietnam and kill as many Vietcongs as possible.

At the other extreme is Maiming Malcolm. He borrows his father's shotgun and shoots off five toes so he will never have to be anything but 4-F for the rest of his life. Between these extremes is much room for the diversity of opinion which makes for exciting classroom dialogue. Each student is asked to place his name on the line which best describes where he fits and to say something about what that line represents to him.

There will be room for the person who argues for going to

Canada to avoid the draft and room for the person who joins ROTC so he can serve as an officer instead of a common foot soldier. As always, the teacher argues that there is no right answer. In the search for values, there must be room for individual choice and the pluralism which makes this society what it is today.

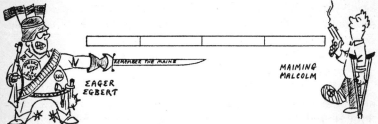

Let's look at a values continuum on racial conflict. This exercise opens up a highly charged topic so it can be discussed with some degree of rationality.

At one extreme we have Super Separatist Sam, whose solution to the race problem is simply to ship every human being back to his original country. He advocates dismembering people whose ancestors came from two different countries. On the other end, we find Multi-Mixing Mike who would insist that all babies be distributed not to their original parents but to couples not of the baby's race. In addition, no couples of the same race can marry, and couples of the same race already married must be divorced and marry outside their race.

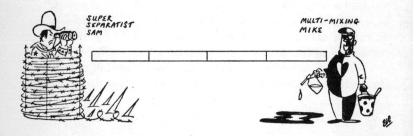

Between these extremes, students must come face-to-face with where they stand on issues of integration, Black Power, de facto segregation, and so on.

CONFRONTATION QUESTIONING

Asking questions is par for the course in the teaching profession. Too often, though, teachers waste their time and their students' time by asking questions for which they have only one answer in mind. We need more value-clarification questions. There is a genuine element of search in such questions, and there is room for diversity.

The strategy of confrontation questioning hits at controversial areas. The tone of these questions is: What is your position? How did you arrive at that value? What other alternatives did you consider? What possibilities are open to you for changing your position, if you should care to do so?

Here is an example. Each student is asked to take out a piece of paper and draw a line down the center. The teacher gives the following directions, allowing time for writing.

List the initials of the people who have come to your house in the past year and who have eaten more than one meal with you. Code these initials with F for friends, R for relatives, O for others.

List the initials of the people whose houses you have gone to for more than one meal in the past year.

1. Which list is longer? Why is it?

2. Put an asterisk beside the initials of the people who make you feel extra good when they walk in the door.

3. Draw a line beneath all of the above data and write out your personal definitions for these words: desegregation, integration, separatism.

4. Without becoming unduly defensive, argue why you are or are not a racist.

5. Discuss the list of initials of those who come to your

house. What does it say about how you live? Do you want to do anything about changing your life?

Confrontation questioning is hard to take lying down. Students become quickly involved. The teacher need do little more than keep students from calling each other names and ask the last part of question 5 often. Everyone needs to be confronted with the gap between what he says and what he does. No one, however, demands that another person do anything to change; the goal is to confront the individual with the simple problem of consistency.

RANK ORDERS

Rank orders get at priorities. They help place our value choices into perspective with possible alternatives. There are no right answers. Each person sees his life from his own set of priorities.

Ask a class to rank order the contributions of these three men in the area of civil rights: Malcolm X, Martin Luther King, Jr., and Dick Gregory. The teacher calls on five or six students, asking them to explain their rankings. Another rank order relates to the eradication of poverty. Ask the students to rank order the following approaches: to destroy all slums in the United States within the next ten years and rebuild them as model cities, to give a guaranteed annual income to those not in the labor force, to see that all schools be legally required to provide an education adequate to life in this society.

These examples are merely suggestive. After awhile, students will bring in their own rank orders to try out on a class. (This keeps a teacher from always hustling his own point of view.) The teacher should always, with quiet dignity, state his own point of view or his own ranking, but he must not control the rank orders to the extent that only his ideas are considered.

Occasionally, it is fun to ask a student for a "fourth" item which he thinks is worse or better than the item he ranked first of the three he was given. There should also be opportunity for a student to change his mind about how he ranked the items, even several weeks later. The principle here is that new facts may change our values.

TIME DIARY

How we spend the twenty-four hours of each day tells, perhaps, more about what we value than anything else. A person does what he values; what he does not value he would be wise not to do. If one has the courage to keep a time diary, the gap between what he says he values and what he actually does about it can be seen all too clearly.

Students are asked to keep the time forms with them at all times during the sampled week. These sheets will not be turned in, so students are urged to make them as personal as possible. The data are gathered in order to locate the sources of one's deepest gratification, discover time use which seems inconsistent with what one says one values, and find those places where one wants to make changes in his life.

Merely adding up the hours one spends on various activities has many advantages. As students compare their classmates' alternative uses of time, they clarify their own values. Usually they see some changes they want to make in their use of time.

AUTOBIOGRAPHICAL QUESTIONNAIRES

We cannot treat lightly the question, "Who am I?" Most people are in desperate search of identity. In this complex and confused world, a self-concept is not so easily handed down by parents or teachers. An autobiographical questionnaire, looked at from year to year, can be one tool for building a self-concept. Below are some questions that have been used successfully in this process:

1. What are some things you really believe in?

2. Where have you spent the best four summers of your life?

3. If you could change your school, what five things would you change?

4. What is the worst work you have done for money?

5. What do you see yourself doing five years from now? Ten years? Twenty?

6. Are there injustices in this community you feel need attention?

7. Do you send any money to charities? Which ones? Which ones will you never send anything to?

8. What are the most important books, movies, plays you've read or seen in the past year?

9. Without mentioning specific names, what are the qualities of the adults whom you respect and admire the most? The least? What are you doing to become more like the former? To keep from being like the latter?

10. Who is your best friend? What do your friends have in common?

11. What are the things you like to do best when you have free time?

12. Have you ever fasted? Would you want that experience?

13. Where do you stand on the Vietnam War? Have you done anything about it?

14. Where do you stand on money, material possessions, and "security"?

15. Do you believe in burial, cremation, or what?

16. What magazines do you subscribe to with your own money?

17. Are you someone who is likely to marry out of your race?

18. What are some of your notions of the good life?

19. Do you wear seat belts?

20. Do you smoke?

21. Do you have full polio protection?

22. What are some of the things you have learned in your search for values in your lifetime?

WEEKLY REACTION SHEETS

The essence of a value-clarification strategy is to get students to examine their lives. A teacher does this, of course, in a non-judgmental, nonmoralizing way. Some good questions are: What was the high point of the week? Were you in emphatic disagreement with anyone this week? Did you institute any changes in your life this week? How could the week have been better? What did you procrastinate about this week? Identify three choices you made this week. Did you make any plans for some future event during the week?

At the end of a six-week period, the teacher should return the reaction sheets. Students may volunteer to talk about any or all of the questions. The teacher should try to summarize the patterns revealed. Students can then help each other find alternatives for more satisfying ways of dealing with the issues raised.

SENSITIVITY MODULES

Another aspect of the action side of valuing is sensitivity modules, which is jargon for a short experience designed to increase awareness.

A class is presented with a list of the following experiences which involve few words, but much action. Class members decide which experiences they want to have first, second, third, and so on. Making their own arrangements, they work their way through the list, meeting each week to compare notes and experiences.

1. Spend a few hours in a prowl car traveling with a team of policemen. Listen to the squad car radio. Ask questions. If the policemen park and walk the beat, walk with them.

2. Sit in the waiting room of the maternity ward of a city hos-

pital whose patients are mostly charity cases. Strike up a conversation with any other persons in the waiting room.

3. Go to a magistrate's court and keep a list of the kinds of cases brought before the magistrate. Who are the customers? How are they handled?

4. Attend church services some Sunday in a storefront church.

5. Borrow a portable tape recorder and interview an elderly citizen who has lived in the neighborhood for ten years or more.

6. Live for three days on the amount of money a typical welfare mother receives to feed a son or daughter closest to your own age.

7. Spend a morning making the rounds with a visiting nurse.

8. Try to call City Hall with a complaint that your landlord did not give you heat, or has not repaired a roof leak, or that the toilet is not working. Better yet, find a neighbor with a real complaint and offer to help him.

9. Go to a local candy store right at the time that a local junior high school is dismissed. Buy a can of soda and sip it slowly while listening and observing.

10. Find a schoolteacher who believes in making home visits and ask if you can go along.

11. Turn off the heat in your own house some night in December or February and spend the night in a cold house.

12. Go to the local campaign headquarters for the Democratic and Republican parties and work for a couple of hours with local people canvassing, leafletting, or making phone calls.

13. Visit an area into which Negroes are just moving. Survey the names of the real estate companies who have signs up. Try to find out if they have been involved in blockbusting in other areas of the city.

14. Work up a lesson on something you think is important

and contact a local junior high school and get permission to teach a group of children your carefully planned lesson.

15. Interview a constable on some recent evictions or repossessions he has handled.

16. Talk to one school dropout and find out what he or she thinks needs to be changed to keep kids in school.

17. Find a housing project and do a tabulation on the toilet facilities provided for the project's three- and four-year-old population, particularly when the children are outside playing.

18. Find a respectable, middle-class Negro (maybe a student in one of your classes) and ask him or her about where he or she is now living and other places he or she has lived. Find out, also, about any experiences he or she has had with real estate agents.

19. Go to one of the little grocery stores in the neighborhood a week before welfare checks come out and note the prices on various staples. Go back the day the checks come out and see if there are any price changes.

20. If you are a male, go get a haircut from a Negro barber.

21. Answer an advertisement in the newspaper for a common laborer job or for assembly work in a factory. Fill out the application blank. Go for the interview.

22. Write and send a letter to the editor of your local paper on any discovery you made during your exposure to these sensitivity modules.

THE ACTION SIDE OF VALUING

Before something can be called a value, you have to do something about it. Action needs to be the final outcome of valuing. The following exercise helps students see alternatives for action.

Write a Letter

1. Write a letter to the editor of your local newspaper. People read these columns more frequently than almost any other

section of the daily newspaper. You *can* influence public opinion.

2. Write a letter to your Congressman or your Senator. Compliment him for something he has done about a problem you are concerned about. Washington *counts* these letters.

3. Send a letter to someone in the news who has done something you respect or admire. You would be surprised how lonely it is to do something different and make the news for doing it.

Attend a Meeting or Organize One

1. Write one of the organizations working for a cause you believe in and ask to be put on the mailing list announcing meetings.

2. Scan the newspapers for announcements of open meetings of groups in which you are interested.

3. Ask your own club, civic group, or church group to have a meeting or invite a guest speaker on a topic you are deeply concerned about.

Take Part in Some Action

1. Distribute leaflets door-to-door or by standing at a subway entrance.

2. Picketing may not be your cup of tea, but it has an impact.

3. Organize a petition drive. Even twenty signatures could make news or cause some public official to take notice.

4. Interview people who have influence. Sometimes just a series of perceptive questions can make an issue come alive.

5. Wear a button.

6. Take part in a peaceful march or other demonstration.

7. Go as a member of a delegation to see some official about some issue.

Face-to-face Acts

1. Speak up for your point of view. (For example, if some-

one says something derogatory about a race or a religion, you can tactfully talk to him about your point of view.)

2. Give someone a pamphlet or an article which argues for a different position than he claims to hold.

3. Try to close the gap between what you say and what you do. Let your life be a living argument for what you believe.

(Remember: All action should be informed action. Consequently, reading, learning, interviewing, discussing, and generally becoming better informed are necessary first steps to *doing* something.)

IN CONCLUSION

These strategies for clarifying values grow out of the book *Values and Teaching* by Louis E. Raths, Merrill Harmin, and Sidney B. Simon. In the book, you will find a rigorous definition of what we mean by values. I have spared you that definition here, but I urge you to read it in this book. Suffice it to say that values demand that we choose, that we know what we prize, and that we do something about it.

ANTICIPATING THE FUTURE

19
A
LITTLE MORE
"KNOW-WHY,"
PLEASE[1]

BY ROBERT W. LYNN

"There has always been something in the American soul" according to literary critic Dwight Macdonald,

> that responds to the how-to book. We are an active, ingenious, pragmatic race concerned . . . with practicality rather than contemplation, with efficiency rather than understanding, with information rather than wisdom. Our frontier past and our industrialized present both incline us toward a preoccupation with technique, with know-how rather than know-why.[2]

This fascination with *techne* has figured prominently in the recent history of Protestant church education. In Victorian America, for example, a few specialists claimed that railroad men made the best Sunday school superintendents. Why? Railroaders know how to run things on time! Later in the early 1900s a host of efficiency experts bombarded church workers with all manner of advice. "This is an age of standardization," one wrote. "The basis of the standard must be practical efficiency." [3] And so the beleaguered Sunday school secretary was encouraged to learn something about statistical theory; meanwhile the superintendent was instructed in the best use of the bell on his desk as a potent reminder of "timeliness," "system," and "intelligent administrative authority." [4] Shortly after World War II, the audio-visual boom in religious education got under way, only to yield to an enthusiasm for group dynamics in the 1950s and 1960s.

And today? The concern about technique is still in evidence. If my reading of the signs of the time is at all correct, the latest contender for attention is *planning*. A major church organization without a "long-range planning committee" or a "planning process" is something of a rarity in liberal Protestant circles. In one sense, of course, there is little that is distinctively new in this emphasis. The older generation in our midst—those whose memories stretch back to the vintage years of the Progressive era—can recall similar appeals for being reasonably precise about "goals," "objectives," and the like. But that hidden continuity is only part of the story. Equally important is the marked difference between past and present.

The educational planners of 1900 or 1915 could concentrate upon "know-how" precisely because they presumed the existence of a common, though unspoken agreement about "know-why." For several decades Sunday school "howtoism" was informed and sustained by a sense of direction, a vision of the intertwined future of the United States and its Protestant churches. Over the last half-century, however, that sort of common-sense knowledge has been gradually fading away in certain sectors of so-called "mainstream" Protestantism. This subtle alteration of ethos poses an extraordinary challenge to aspiring, liberal church planners. Their problem goes deeper than just an adoption of the latest planning techniques, borrowed from the Pentagon, business schools or the corporate managers. The root of the matter lies in the search for a hopeful future.

In order to understand the newness of the current situation, a historical flashback to pre-Civil War America is necessary.

Our evangelical forefathers' "know-why" sprang in large part out of their vision of a distinctive destiny. For many of these folk, living in the early nineteenth century, the future was promising—in fact, brilliant, because of America. They could not speak for long of their own religious future without also thinking of the United States and its special role in God's providential work.

In the last five years I have been plodding through the mountainous literature of educational publications written by Protestants in the stretch of years between the War of 1812 and the firing of the first shot at Fort Sumter in 1861. It makes fascinating reading for anyone who is interested in understanding the lure of the future for past generations. The material is rich in diversity—for instance, the annual reports of the American Sunday School Union, one of the nerve centers of the Sunday school movement in the national period; sermons concerning the necessity to "civilize" the new Americans on the frontier; tracts that plead for support of burgeoning colleges and seminaries.

What could justify the energy and sacrifices necessary to launch these new enterprises? In part the evangelicals appealed to the imperative of accepting their responsibilities as inhabitants of the Protestant Zion. Americans, so they believed, had been delivered out of the Babylonian captivity of the Old World into life in the "New Israel." One of the better-selling items in the libraries offered by the American Sunday School Union was a life of George Washington in which the founding father was portrayed as a Moses who had led his people to the land of milk and honey. Moreover, the landscape itself was considered to be a reminder of God's providence. The mountains, valleys and plains—these moral and educational forces constituted an ideal matrix for the nurturing of a new race, open to the Lord's future.

America was not only the beginning of something new; its presence also signified the coming of the final stage of history. These Protestants disagreed among themselves about the imminence of the millennium and, even more important, about whether or not it would come before the Advent of Christ. But whatever their differences, they were largely united in the conviction that they stood on the threshold of an extraordinarily important era. The most decisive future man had ever experienced was about to unfold. It would become evident first in the New World and then in other less favored parts of the world. This meant, among other things, that American Protestantism had a special responsibility as a missionary force both within this nation and to the world. The logic of the mission: Christianize the United States so that it, in turn, can lead the way in Christianizing the world. In this notion—so flatly stated here as to be incomprehensible, much less acceptable, to many Christians living in the last part of the twentieth century—lay the impulse of hope, the source of urgency and quickening expectancy that inspired evangelical educators during those early formative years.

To be sure, there were other forces at work in the minds of these innovators. They were also prompted by the ever-present reality of collective self-interest. In the wake of disestablishment after the Revolutionary War, the evangelicals had to develop a new generation of institutions for passing on the Christian faith. Otherwise the Protestant presence in the new nation would have slowly withered away. They were not about to let that happen! A host of other factors—their corrosive hatred of a growing Roman Catholic community, a distrust of the native "infidels" in their midst, and denominational competition—also aroused them to prodigious effort. But none of these motivations, even when cloaked in appropriate ideological disguise, could have provided the requisite rationale and justification for their developing educational strategy. It was their vision of the future, more than anything else, that vindicated the demands they were making upon themselves and others.

The ensuing creation was a marvel of complexity. In the early decades of the nineteenth century these churchmen patched together a new pattern—or ecology—of Protestant educational institutions. By a series of apparent coincidences they devised a variety of ways through which America could be prepared for its future.

1. Foremost among these educational institutions was the *revival*. That judgment may surprise the latter-day observer whose impressions of this form are largely governed by his reactions to Billy Graham's technectronic spectaculars. In the national period, however, the revival often functioned as the great school of the Protestant public. In that setting all sorts of educational activity was observable, i.e., the deliberate forming of a community and its self-identity, the shaping of values, attitudes and beliefs, etc.

2. An allied institution was the *Sunday school*. As Elliott Wright and I have tried to indicate in *The Big Little School*, this transplanted American version of the English charity school served a variety of disparate purposes. Its foremost function, in the judgment of its evangelical proponents, was to provide a context for conversion so that the next generation could take up the work of a missionary nation. Although these Sunday school pioneers were seldom optimistic enough to think this purpose would ever be fully realized, they still expected that somewhere on every Sunday another recruit would have been enlisted in the army of the Lord.

3. The evangelicals relied upon *publications* as another educational medium. For example, the American Bible Society and the American Tract Society were among the leading publishers of the time. Meanwhile, the Sunday School Union sold or gave away minilibraries to thousands of hamlets along the Western frontier. The evangelical literature ranged from pocket Bibles and tracts to etiquette books on "How to Be a

Christian Gentleman." (If the latter reference sounds frivolous and irrelevant in a discussion about education, then I ask you to reflect on the educative power—for better or worse—of such current magazines as *Cosmopolitan* and *Playboy*.)

4. During the same period the evangelicals took the lead in spawning *denominational colleges,* a creation that was somewhat different from the colonial college in ethos and purpose.

5. In a parallel move they also developed the *confessional seminary.* No longer were these churchmen content to rely upon the colleges and the apprentice system for theological training. Andover and Princeton became the model for this new educational venture in the United States.

6. All of these schools were encouraged and sustained by benevolent agencies and Sunday school societies which eventually evolved into the first approximation of the *denominational board of education* as we know it today.

7. Although the emerging *public school* could not be officially described as part of the Protestant ecology, evangelical leaders often praised it fondly as a Christian outpost in a society which was increasingly besieged by strangers from abroad.

8. Finally, *family* and *congregational life* were also counted upon as significant educational contexts.

There, in brief, is the outline form of a potent educational ecology. No self-conscious strategist mapped it out as whole; no committee said, "Now this is what we must do." It came into existence in a haphazard, unplanned manner. Each of its expressions represents an ad hoc response to a particular need or opportunity. But what held it together, once it was established in the routines of Protestant church life, was the evangelical spirit, a spirit roused and enlivened by the conviction that at least here in America Christians were on the verge of entering God's future. For here they were planting the seed of the posterity of a New Adam in the rich, virgin soil of Eden, warmed by the Sun of righteousness.

This dream about an American Adam is still alive in some quarters of Protestantism. Look, if you will, well to the "right" on the denominational spectrum, and there you will find the traditional ecology still intact. The more strenuous of the evangelical groups maintain both the spirit and institutional forms of a bygone era. Further to the "left," however, we can discern increasing flounderings and difficulties. Liberal Protestants continue to rely upon the old pattern of Sunday school-seminary-denominational board of education, etc.— but without the same enthusiasm or conviction so evident among the evangelicals.

Yet this educational ecology represents only the visible portion of our inheritance from nineteenth-century Protestantism. What happens to its invisible counterpart may be of far greater importance. I doubt that the old evangelical image of the future will play the same role that it did earlier in this century. Historian Henry F. May once commented that Americans in the early 1900s looked to the "unfolding American future" as the "main guarantee of universal morality." [5] So it has been until quite recently. From Woodrow Wilson's crusade to make the world safe for democracy to the inaugural address of John F. Kennedy, Americans have been entreated to bear the burdens of a secular missionary nation. Then came the Vietnam debacle. And after Vietnam, what? No one knows for sure. My own guess is that it will be far harder for most Americans to revert to an earlier state of innocence. Our confidence in America as Zion has been damaged, if not destroyed. It will probably never be quite the same again.

That makes the immediate future of liberal Protestant education all the more uncertain. Despite its appearance of modernity and relentless relevance, "mainstream" Protestantism is rooted in the ethos of the last century. Whenever that foundation is shaken, the reverberations rattle the present structure. Few liberals can escape the sounds of these rumblings.

Do we have the courage to acknowledge the shaking of the

foundations? That is the question before us in the 1970s. The present voguish interest in planning could be a sophisticated way of blocking out such discordant noises from the deep. If that happens, another chapter will have been written in the disappointing love affair of American Protestantism with "know-how." I do not know any shortcuts to answers about "know-why." In that pain, however, lies the promise of a new beginning. If some of those planning committees now scattered across the country—whether in the inner sanctums of a denominational board, congregation or seminary—can persist in wanting to know why, then perhaps there will be glimmerings of a new future along the horizon.

A little more "know-why," if you please.

20
PREDICAMENTS AND POINTERS IN RELIGIOUS EDUCATION

BY RANDOLPH CRUMP MILLER

It has been said that people were not really devout in the Middle Ages in spite of the profundity of some of the theologians. About 1800 at Yale, only about 3 percent of the students admitted to being Christian. It has been some time since Nietzsche announced the death of God, a theme which Rubenstein stressed after considering Hitler's massacre of the Jews. Yet we are only a decade or so beyond the optimism of piety on the Potomac, when we had burgeoning Sunday schools and expensive curriculum materials that promised a rosy future.

I don't think we expect history to repeat itself or run in cycles, and yet there is a constant reassertion of many fundamental themes as we move from one decade to another. We go back in history and pick up something that had been jettisoned because it looks useful again. We get caught in predicaments and someone comes up with a new pointer (which may have had previous effectiveness in an older model) and we move from pessimism to hope.

Certainly the predicament of religious education today is serious on several levels. Catholics may be more cheerful about some aspects of their educational procedures than

Protestants or Jews, but their parochial schools are in difficulty. Secular educators may be more hopeful than religious educators, but even in this affluent country education may become so costly we cannot afford it. Christians and Jews alike are suffering from confusion over the nature of faith. Religious institutions are reexamining their purposes and are not sure of their identity. Professional religious educators are either suffering from an identity crisis or are vanishing. Because we have not learned to distinguish between education and indoctrination, we have become even more unsure about methods. Let us look at these predicaments and see if there is a basis for hope.

I. As I look back at theological developments during my lifetime, we have not had much consensus in our belief systems. Liberalism and fundamentalism, empiricism and neo-orthodoxy, traditionalism and relevance, the death of God and the rise of a new-classical theism are just examples of the conflicts. The World Council of Churches or Vatican II may have come up with irenic statements, but they did not catch the imagination. The younger generation is moving from social radicalism toward either mysticism or a naïve Jesus-ism, but this development is in a state of flux.

In the meantime, some religious educators have moved with the winds of opinion and made what seem to many leaders to be real advances, and others have stayed within a traditional stance with uniform lessons and the Baltimore catechism. And whenever the going gets tough for those who emphasize the newer ideas, there is a retreat to previously held positions. Thus a "Maginot Line" consciousness has developed in many churches and synagogues, resulting in students who are ready to face the nineteenth century!

There is a deeper level of this crisis of faith. Harvey Cox got close to it in *The Secular City*. The operative mind of the average church or synagogue attender is formed by living in a metropolis and he makes his decisions on a secular level. He carries an umbrella rather than prays for good weather. He doesn't expect the sun to stand still but can watch someone go to the moon. If he gets some water from the Jordan River for a sentimental baptism, he knows that the water will be polluted. His world view is formed by the scientific mind, and if religion is to have any meaning it must be in terms which the scientific mind can grasp. Such a mind has difficulty with poetry, myth, folklore, and other language games which religious people play.

From the point of view of the historian, however, it has always been this way. The naturalism of some Greek philosophers and the evolutionary theories of Darwin posed similar questions, yet the belief systems of most Christians and Jews survived in altered form. We learned to read the Bible from different perspectives, and even unconsciously we learned to demythologize passages that did not match current scientific views. But never have we had a wide consensus of theological views.

One way out is the discovery that all belief systems are relative, human, and elusive, but that they point in a direction that shows us the reality of God. We can become excited about some of the younger generation in their rediscovery of the magical, the holy, the mysterious element that provides sources of strength and courage and guidance in a confused world. If we realize that all belief systems are pointing at a reality that cannot be captured, that worship of the holy is an empirical anchor for such systems of belief, and that the capacity to point is the basis for education, we may develop a belief system or systems that can operate effectively in the future. Then we can begin to reflect on what it is all about and develop ethical insights for social and personal guidance.

II. The predicament of religious institutions (churches, synagogues, and schools) reflects that of our belief systems. First of all, there is the question of authority. If there is an official belief system, who is bound to accept it? Even the pronouncements of the pope are rejected by many Catholics—priests as well as lay people. Protestant churches have made social policy statements that have led not only to rejection but to economic boycott of the parish or denomination. The expectation that a sermon will be taken at face value has long since passed.

When the church is right, it lacks authority; when it is wrong, it lacks credibility, and this is a greater crisis. In 1840 the workmen in Sheffield, England, saw clearly that the bishops voted with the owners against labor, and the churches lost their laboring class. Consistently the churches have favored the status quo, have aligned themselves with conservative political movements, have been opposed to scientific theories, have found ways to support slavery, racism, continued poverty, and nondemocratic forms of government.

What is worse, the churches have simply been irrelevant. When someone pronounces that an attitude is "Sunday school stuff," we recognize the force of this criticism. The artificiality of Sunday school and parochial school morality has nothing to do with the business of daily living. There seems to be a majority of lay people who are happy with this irrelevance and who are opposed to any kind of stance or action with economic, political, or social significance. Religious institutions that act out their convictions on political matters may be threatened by the government, especially in terms of tax exemption.

On the other hand, religious institutions that take seriously their responsibilities in the secular world are in danger of losing their religious roots. When social or moral decisions and actions are seen in a secular perspective, it does not matter about belief systems and religious dimensions. The religious person becomes uneasy about social action because he has a vague intuition that it is not grounded in worship.

One way to get at this complicated dilemma is to realize that moral and social systems are not absolute. Just as our belief systems are tentative and open to constant change, so moral decisions are based upon conditions that are constantly changing. Yet both theology and morality are based upon the degree of knowledge that we have, and therefore they represent truth as far as we can have it in human terms. If our religious outlook is grounded in the relationship with God as a living reality, our theological opinions and moral decisions will be somewhat tentative but sufficiently certain for us to act upon them. This is the point at which faith, risk, and courage become factors in religious and moral behavior.

Religious institutions are going to become more democratic. Already there is rebellion on the part of some lay people because they object to the assertion of authority or to the particular statements of church leaders or committees. Many Catholics, for example, reject the authority of the pope in the area of contraception. Protestants may reject or support statements or actions by the World Council of Churches. This kind of response, it seems to me, is proper when it is grounded in informed conviction, and this is where religious education has a profound responsibility.

If we begin with the assumption that belief systems and moral decision-making are open to criticism and improvement because they are man-made, then careful examination of factual knowledge and critical reflection are essential to religious education. There is still a large place for history and tradition to help us understand the present, but authority will be interpreted in its basic meaning of moral persuasion, which is both trustworthy and living in its hold upon men. Once the coercive and dogmatic elements of so-called authority are excised, it has a proper place in religious education. Then the institution can regain both its credibility and its relevance.

III. We are in the midst of a reconsideration of the function of the professional religious educator. The predicament has reached almost crisis proportions in terms of opportunities and jobs. Even some theological seminaries are eliminating teachers in this field. Somehow, it is assumed, students for the ministry will learn about religious education by some kind of osmosis. This reflects the confusion in terms of the function and role of the religious educator. Professional religious educators in churches and synagogues are not sure of their roles, and they suffer from a lack of status. Teachers of religion are not sure of their goals; in some situations they are responsible for indoctrination and conversion; in others they are charged to teach religion objectively (and it is not clear what this means). Furthermore, all religious educators are caught up in the confusion in belief systems and in the predicament of the religious institution. I wonder sometimes if they are also suffering from a failure of nerve, for the demands on the religious educator are great and the cooperation received is slight.

The professional religious educator has always had a hard time. It is a new profession, going back only to the beginning of this century. Most of those who formed the Religious Education Association in 1903 were not technically trained in education or religious education. During the past seventy years the number of professionals increased greatly, probably hitting its peak in the 1920s and 1930s. The national departments of religious education had their greatest power in the 1950s. But the influence of the professional educators never reached a majority of the churches and synagogues, which were more interested in indoctrination and tradition than in education as such. It is out of this conflict between education and evangelism that the present malaise has developed.

There are some pointers toward the future, however, that provide a basis for hope. First, it is obvious that church and synagogue need education for their survival, and survival is something that religious institutions are good at. Second, as a domesticated educational system begins to move toward its implications for living, such concepts as liberation and revolution begin to enter the picture, along with conflict within the institution. If the ferment in belief systems and religious institutions begins to provide new enthusiasm in these directions (as in the thought of Paulo Freire), religious educators may be caught up in a liberation movement within the institutions. We saw the beginnings of this in the support by some white and black churches of the black liberation movement. Third, there is the impact of the younger generation in at least two points: the rediscovery of the mystical element in all religions from Zen and Hinduism to westernized Christianity, and the recovery of Jesus as a source of power—both of these may be combined with the more secular approach to social and political change coming from the revolution in morals.

The professional religious educator needs to rethink his role in terms of these developments. He will be working within churches and synagogues and schools to enable students to see that the certainty of religion lies in a relationship with God through his fellows and nature, and that belief systems, moral decisions, and religious institutions are significant as man's ways of appropriating religious insights for meaningful personal and social living. This is one way of speaking of "conscientization" as coming to awareness of what it means to be religious in the modern world.

IV. We face one other predicament: our understanding of method. Here we can be helped greatly by research into religious and moral development and by new theories of method being developed by secular educators. Obviously, the methods used in the past leave much to be desired. They led frequently into the bind of a fixed belief system, an authoritative institution, and a paralysis in the profession of religious education. Methods, content, and theological convictions go together, and because we had an inadequate view of theology and institutions, we got caught in transmissive methods that failed to lead to increased capacity to think and act in terms of our religious profession. Morality was tied to religious beliefs in such a manner that both moral insight and belief systems were fossilized. If one rejected this static view of religion, he was not provided with a dynamic alternative but only with the negative conclusion that God is dead.

The mammoth volume edited by Merton Strommen on *Research on Religious Development* (New York: Hawthorn, 1971) puts much of the research in perspective. The significance of Piaget as indicated by Goldman and Bull provides us with knowledge of the development of conceptual thinking in religion and morals, so that we can develop an understanding of methods that fits the research findings, and thus we can move forward into more fruitful research into the adequacy of methods. But the fixation on any method is just as dangerous as the static elements in belief systems and institutions. Any method that connects content with the learner so that he is initiated into a value system (that also is not fixed) is valid for that purpose. Any method that stimulates the art of thinking and the analysis of decision-making is suitable. Any method that assists the learner to be liberated from false choices and inadequate evaluation of himself as a person is to be chosen over a method that denies these aims. Thus the method is significant in terms of the nature of man and of God as well as in effectiveness in learning. Certain kinds of training which may be effective on man are only suitable for dogs and mice because they fail to treat the learner as human beings.

In the future, then, we may move away from the typical school-room approach for some purposes and stay within it for others. We may have careful analysis of subject matter as a discipline in itself, and we may have experiments with life on the parkway. We may find that Bible quizzes are fun, but discover at the same time that there is nitroglycerine in the Bible story that when appropriated may blow up traditional ways of doing things. We may preach from time to time on the good news and we may scold and prophesy and promise, but we will also enter into relationships with the preached at on a level of discussion and criticism. We may analyze religious language so that we know what language game we are playing, and then use any language game that promises to communicate. We may work for conversion and commitment and seek to evoke insights like our own, and then be happy as the learner makes his own decisions which are not like ours.

I see a more free and flexible type of religious education in churches and synagogues, schools and colleges. I see some parents being drawn into such a system (if it is a system) and sharing similar goals. Out of such an open approach may come not only new disclosures and commitments but action on a broad front from the personal to the moral. But I do not see any bed of roses. I see conflict, holding back, and open opposition both within and outside the church. I see the reassertion of nineteenth-century theology and methods, nostalgia for the old-line Sunday school and the dogmatic nun in the parochial school. I see people turning away from the churches and synagogues, so that the percentage of people in religious institutions will be a smaller proportion of the population; and I see other institutions which are alive and attractive and bubbling over with enthusiasm (being in God) to carry out the mission of the church in society. In some mysterious way, God is at work in the processes of religious education, or else the results from our bumbling efforts would not be as fruitful.

So I see predicaments and pointers, and for me the pointers do not eliminate the predicaments; but out of the conflict comes a strong element of hope that we will keep our belief systems and institutions in proper perspective and open to what is new, and that religious educators will clarify their identities and roles in the near future. Cycles go up and down, and when there is genuine concern for what it is all about, sooner or later there is an upward swing.

21
ASKING THE RIGHT QUESTIONS

BY RACHEL HENDERLITE

Church School Superintendent: Well, we've gotten all the teachers lined up for the fall.

Pastor: Congratulations!

Church School Superintendent: But I'm not sure it's worth it.

Pastor: Then, why don't we call it off?

Church School Superintendent: Oh no! We can't do that! We've got to have a Sunday school!

This conversation represents the ambivalence and chaos marking Christian education today. It is probably repeated every summer in churches around the country. C. Ellis Nelson, in a recent article, said outright that Christian education is in a demoralized state. Church school attendance is dropping. Young people are turned off by the church. Congregations are puzzled and keep asking questions about possible solutions to the problem. But the confusion is most clearly seen in the fact that the questions being asked are undoubtedly the wrong questions: Shall we do away with the church school and set up weekday classes instead? Shall we purchase different curriculum resources? Shall we build a new educational plant? Shall we stop using laymen and use only professionally trained, paid teachers?

To ask these questions is to assume that we are doing the right thing and merely need to do it better. It is to ask the questions of method, without having asked the more fundamental questions of purpose: Is what we are doing right? Is this what the church ought to be about? For it is possible that the pattern of Christian education we have used unquestioningly over the years is not the most useful way of doing the job of Christian education today.

The recent, highly significant book *The Big Little School*, by Robert W. Lynn and Elliott Wright (New York: Harper & Row, 1971), is a graphic study of two hundred years of the Sunday school in this country. The authors point out the powerful influence the Sunday school has had on American life as "the training ground of American Protestantism." Despite increasing attacks upon it, the Sunday school continues to thrive; and despite efforts to change it, it has continued in much the same form as fifty years ago.

The significance of this work by Lynn and Wright for us is the authors' insight that the Sunday school was developed as an expression of nineteenth-century evangelical Protestantism and seems unable to thrive in any other theological climate. The churches that are having the greatest response to the Sunday school today—the Assembly of God, the Pentecostal Holiness churches, the Southern Baptists—are the churches that continue to profess the fundamentalist, nineteenth-century evangelistic Christianity out of which the church school sprang. The management of the Sunday school by comparatively uneducated laymen, the uncritical acceptance of scripture as the literal Word of God, the simple, unsophisticated doctrine of individual "salvation"—all of these have been characteristic of the Sunday school from the beginning and continue to make it a superb instrument for mission of the church as these communions have understood it.

The churches often spoken of as "the main-line Protestant churches," however, have had less success with Sunday school enrollment and are being driven to question whether the Sunday school is suited to the educational task as it must now be defined. Changes in the world and in the church have made it impossible for these communions to maintain the simplistic approach to Christian education that has been most congenial to the Sunday school movement. The growth of cities, the development of technology, and the rise of the massive industrial-governmental-military complex have made almost irrelevant the individualistic thrust of nineteenth-century evangelical Protestantism. Moreover, the development of scientific or "critical" study of scripture, the general uneasiness with the fundamentalistic emphasis on personal purity and "a happy world up yonder" and the development of the ecumenical movement with its increased attention to the nature of the church and the relationship of church and world— all these factors seem to demand another look at church education.

To point out these wide differences in American Protestantism and the fact that the Sunday school seems more "successful" in the conservative churches than in the more liberal ones is not to belittle either branch of the church. It is not intended to declare one branch of the church better than another. Nor is there any intent here to belittle the Sunday school. The Sunday school has had a powerful impact upon the life of the nation, as Lynn and Wright show, and cannot be dismissed lightly. It may be important, however, to recognize differences in the views of the church's nature and mission that are held by different parts of the church and to suggest that each congregation, if it is to be effective, must examine its own convictions and adopt the kind of school that is best suited to education in accordance with these convictions.

Our problem in Christian education has been what Charles E. Silberman in his critique of public education has called "mindlessness," "the failure to think seriously about purpose or consequence."

> In an era of radical change such as the present, no approach is more impractical than one which takes the present arrangements and practices as given, asking only, "How can we do what we are now doing more effectively?" or "How can we bring the worst institutions up to the level of the best?" These questions need to be asked, to be sure; but one must also realize that the best may not be good enough and may, in any case, already be changing.[1]

The crisis of education in the main-line Protestant churches calls for stringent self-examination: for asking the most basic questions about the church's nature and mission, for assessing the congregation's current program and its present organizational patterns in the light of that nature and mission. The answers to these questions will vary widely among the various communions. It is possible that the shape of the questions will vary as widely. But the congregation may not with impunity accept the answers other congregations have found and busy itself with all the activities these congregations regard as useful means to their ends; nor may it hang on to practices and structures that have been found useful in other times. Each congregation must ask basic questions about the church, and only when the answers to these questions are clear may the congregation begin to ask educational questions. The questions to be asked by the congregation that is concerned about its educational program, then, are such questions as the following.

What is distinctive about the Christian church? What peculiar beliefs and practices give us our reason for being? What is distinctive about this congregation? What do we believe about

God? What do we understand as our history and destiny? To what end has God called us?

Does this congregation have responsibility for the community in which God has placed us? Or does God intend that we separate ourselves from the community as a holy people? If the former, what is it God wants for this community? How may we act so that we do not block his will but act to help bring it about?

And then: How can we equip our people for becoming responsible members of this congregation of called people? How is faith elicited in another? What facts of our heritage and culture do these people need in order to understand and accept their own identity as "children of the covenant"? What skills do they need to become and continue to be responsible, committed disciples of Christ in a world of crisis and revolution? What do we mean by "the freedom for which Christ set us free"? How does a man receive the freedom not to be conformed to the world, the freedom to explore the meaning of the gospel for the particular situations in which their lives will be lived, the freedom to be transformed by the gospel?

These are the first questions to be asked: questions of the essence of the church, its origin, its nature, its intention; questions about the nature of personal faith; the meaning of salvation; the nature of God's forgiving grace; the operation of the Holy Spirit. Having pushed these questions to their limit and having arrived at answers that we can maintain with some integrity, we are ready for the more familiar questions: How do people develop the understanding and skills that we have identified as essential for living as a follower of Christ in an alien world? What kind of skills will adults need in order to help children develop the understandings and skills they will need?

Then and only then come the questions of materials and strategy, the questions we so often start with and never get away from:

What kind of classrooms does this congregation need? What materials and supplies? What schedule is most convenient for our different classes? Do we need slide and filmstrip projectors? A school library? Shall we have workers' conferences and teacher-training classes? Shall we set up labs, observation centers, workshops? For what? Shall we use the discovery-learning method?

Our failure to ask the basic questions first causes us to overlook the limited function of a "school" in the total ministry of the church and so to distort the entire meaning of school. In all too many instances, congregations count on the church school to provide the child or the youth with the chief or only encounter he will have with the Christian faith, and then they are surprised when young people drop out and children attend with dragging feet. If this is what is taking place in your congregation, you may be sure that the fault is not lack of filmstrip projectors or the choice of the wrong curriculum material. The fault lies with the congregation's own faith and life. It is safe to surmise that nothing exciting enough is happening among the adults to arouse questions deep enough for young people to ask. They don't see that they *need* a school. They have seen nothing worth studying. Whatever facts or doctrines we give them in church school are, insofar as they know, without meaning for the drugs, the premarital sex, the apathy, and all the other phenomena of this age that are going on at the high school across the street. They seem to the young person to offer no equipment for life on the university campus or in the business world. Whatever "faith" young people see reflected in sober hymns and liturgies on a Sunday morning at eleven o'clock seems to have no bearing on the community's stubborn resistance to the claims of black Americans and Mexican-Americans for decent housing, an equal education, and fair employment practices. It seems to have no bearing on Vietnam.

Suppose a congregation were to define faith in Jesus

Christ, as I believe it could, as a community's response to God as revealed in Jesus Christ, and suppose it demonstrated such a faith in its life. Any person coming into contact with this faith might come to accept God as the most real factor in life. He would know that he himself and indeed the whole world was brought into being by God, and that the course of history is under the control of God. He would mean by "God" a supernatural being with ultimate power who is at work to bring the whole world into his family, who intends that men should be free to shape their own destinies in part and to have some effect on the course of history. He would know that this God yearns to transform the hearts of men with his grace so that they are free to relate to other beings, including God himself, and free to be his instrument through Jesus Christ in the transformation of the structures of society. In the light of such faith the person might know a great hope, a great exhilaration, for his own life and for the course of history. He might be excited about taking his place in the community as a member of the transformed and transforming body of folk called by God for service to the world in the name of God's own Son. All of his decisions and responses would then in some measure be affected by this new image of himself and of the universe brought to him as part of his own faith by the faith of the believing community.

Probably no congregation would define faith in just the words that I have used here. In fact, what I have said in the preceding paragraph may be actually offensive to you. If so, try working out your own statement of what a transforming faith might be like. And if you believe the educational work of the church has anything to do with shaping this faith, you will already have a clue to the nature of education in the church.

Your primary question, then, would be: How would one elicit this kind of faith in a child or an adult? Obviously not by sitting him down in a proportioned chair with a group of his peers and reciting to him the creeds of the church at 9:30

every Sunday morning for an hour or so. Especially if nobody who is important to him acts as if the creeds were significant. The least psychologically oriented of us knows that the profound belief that interprets a person's basic relationship to reality is not brought about by the ability to repeat a doctrinal statement affirmed by another. We do not know a great deal about how learning takes place, and we would do well not to speak dogmatically about it. But it seems clear that "education into faith" is not the function of a school. It is rather a function of the whole congregation as the congregation is moved by the Holy Spirit. In my own judgment, the only way in which such faith as this can be elicited is through inclusion in a community of faith where the whole life of the community is shaped and governed by the community's commitment to its Lord.

The congregation's responsibility for nurture in the faith lies in the fact that God does not seem to have provided any instrument that can take the place of the believing community as a medium for the work of the Holy Spirit. As a person is included in the congregation of believers, he is exposed to the Holy Spirit through the congregation's own fullness. He worships with the congregation and becomes aware of the living presence of God speaking to his people through word and sacrament, and being spoken to in prayer and hymn and liturgy. He observes individuals and groups struggling with the decisions they have to make in areas of their responsibility. He perceives their faith in the reality and nearness of God and their concern to interpret each situation in the light of Jesus Christ. He watches their final decision-making and the action that follows decision. He hears their prayer for forgiveness as they fall short of grasping the full meaning of God's intention in the situation and their prayer for his transforming and redeeming grace.

He comes to know—in a subtle way—that to these people who make up the congregation the most real factor in the situation is God, that they understand their own behavior to be always contingent upon him and in response to him. So, he is introduced to faith. As he participates with these men of faith, he is himself drawn into the faith, and he is on the way to becoming himself a man or woman of faith.

Then he is ready for a school. Then he has questions to ask: How did we get to be this kind of people, when obviously not everyone looks at life in this way? How did we come to know that God is like this? How will I be sure that these people are right about him? How did I happen to be included in their fellowship? What would it mean for me if I were to reject it? How will I have to act if I accept their convictions?

And when he asks these questions, he is ready to sit down with his peers and, together with a wise man or woman of the faith, study the origins and meanings of the Christian faith. But it is the reality of the faith that he has already perceived and that is beginning to take hold of him that is worth studying about.

The church's school is the church's agency in which the church makes provision for the study of the Word of God—for itself and for its children. Here it enters into consistent study of the ground of its faith, week after week returning to the exploration of scripture, in which it believes God had spoken and continues to speak. For it knows that its life is nourished by the Word and depends on the Word.

Moreover, it is convinced that the emerging faith of its children will come to maturity only through reflection on God and the work of God in history. The fragile faith of the child requires understanding of its grounding in the gracious acts of God in history if it is to become more than a childish faith. Faith has its intellectual tasks to do. It must know the ground on which it stands; it must reflect upon the nature and intentions of God; it must explore new ways of worshiping; and it must attempt to discern the meaning of obedience to God in a radically contemporary world.

But the school will take different forms according to the congregation's need. *When* it meets is not important. What gadgets it has or does not have are of little importance. The significant thing is to recognize the school of the church as the occasion for men and women of faith to come together with their children to reflect upon the meaning of these events in human history through which God has made himself known and through which he has called this fellowship of faith into being. If the congregation to which you belong does not have this kind of conviction about God and about itself, and this kind of excitement about life, it just may be that the Sunday school superintendent will be right in wanting to forget about the school of the church.

22
THE CHURCH AND FUTURE: AN EDUCATIONAL PERSPECTIVE

BY LETTY M. RUSSELL

WHY SHOULD THE CHURCH BE INTERESTED IN THE FUTURE?

The church comes by its interest in the future very naturally. It lives in a modern world of change and it lives by the biblical promise of God's future for all mankind. The world in which we live today is changing so fast that we live in the future all the time. In the nineteenth century men became fascinated with history because they discovered that they could make events as well as things. In the twentieth century men are becoming fascinated with the future because they have discovered that events in a world of constant change can be fashioned only by a study of history of the future as well as the past and present.

The purpose of this study of the future, or *futurology* as it has come to be called, is to shape the future and prevent it from just happening as fate. Technological forecasts of our future capability of self-destruction by bomb, pollution, genetics, etc. point to the fact that the church as part of society must be concerned about the future if there is to be one at all.

Of course, the church has always been concerned about the future because of the biblical promise of the future. The Bible is full of expectation, often embarrassingly so. This expectation of the fulfillment of God's plan for the establishment of his kingdom is usually called *eschatology* (thinking about last things, or the end). Even before the events of the New Testament, the Hebrew people were thinking in a futuristic mode as they lived by faith in a God of Promise whose redeeming action was known in the events of history. Christian theology and the future have always belonged together also, because the good news about Jesus of Nazareth is that God has decisively intervened in history and the life of mankind and established his promise of a New Age.

Today the church continues its concern for the future as modern theology seeks out the meaning of this Christian hope and tries to express it through concrete concern for the world of change. The church shares responsibility with all communities of good will everywhere who see the need for planning and intervention in the social changes of today so that the future will be one of freedom and justice for all mankind.

CHURCH PARTICIPATION
IN PLANNING THE FUTURE

The church can participate in planning the future by recognizing the way in which theology and futurology can interact in a process of hoping and planning. Theology is most concerned with the *anticipation* of the future. It writes its scenarios or stories of the future on the basis of the experience of Jesus Christ both in the past and present which points to the future. In order to realize that future when all men might live in the kind of harmony, love, and humanity which Jesus established, Christians are called to live *now as if* that future is already in our midst. Our actions as Christians anticipate the future by showing forth the Lord and his promise now in service, fellowship, and celebration. The work of the Messiah and therefore of the Messianic people is to anticipate the future now by pointing to places where the lame walk, the blind see, and the poor have good news preached to them. When this future happens in little ways in our lives, we give thanks and rejoice that the perspective of hope is being fulfilled.

Futurology as an emerging science of the future is most concerned with *projecting* the future. It writes its scenarios or stories of the future on the basis of trends of the past and present projected or extrapolated into the future. Feeding vast quantities of data into computers and analyzing the hunches of countless experts, it is able to tell us *when* something is likely to happen, *if* it happens. Such forecasts can stretch from negative utopias, and horrible destruction, to when disposable clothing will come on the market, or when man may expect to live in a leisure society. The purpose of these forecasts of the future is to enable interested groups in business, industry, government, etc. to be able to plan possible alternative futures and to choose those futures which seem most valuable to those doing the planning.

In spite of their differences, theologians and futurologists share a common task. This task is that of *intervention* in the future on behalf of all mankind. For the Christian the concern to intervene stems from a perspective of hope in God and his plan for justice, freedom, and humanity for the world. For the futurologist it may stem from a variety of motives or values which lead him to pick out from many forecasts the one forecast which seems the most likely or the most important for future development. Nevertheless, *hoping and planning* should go together. Hoping (theology) needs planning (futurology) in order to make it concrete and to spell out specific actions for changing the world according to a vision of new humanity. Planning needs hoping to provide the vision and energy which is necessary to work out plans, for the values by which choices of future are made have become a crucial issue in our time.

THE PURPOSE OF CHURCH INVOLVEMENT
IN FUTURES PLANNING

All of us should seek to involve ourselves in planning and shaping the future. As one person quipped, "I'm interested in the future; I'm going to spend the rest of my life there." Whether we become involved at the level of our professions, or of social action, or of local or national study and pressure groups, study of the future and planning for the future is the only way to make sure we have a future worth living in.

Futures planning is one way in which the church can participate with God in his concern for the future of society. It calls for people who are willing to *work on concrete planning programs* such as the White House Conference on Children and Youth. Christians are called to join with all others in society who are concerned for the aspects of freedom and education which affect the "software" (the human factors) of society. Otherwise, it appears that the "hardware" (technological factors) will determine man's destiny.

Besides actual participation in planning, another purpose of the church's involvement in futurology is that of *arousing and crystallizing public opinion.* At the moment, most futurology is done by the military-industrial complex. Such planning tends to operate as fate and produce a military-industrial future. Our society needs countless groups of aware and informed citizens who can bring pressure to bear on behalf of the poor, uneducated, defuturized of society. These groups should come to understand the planning process and how futurology is done so that they can press the government to invest money in human concerns. A good example of the amount of public awareness and pressure needed to force action against special interest groups is the current overdue campaign against pollution. Such a campaign is desperately needed in such areas as educational reform, race, women's liberation, national policies concerning the Third World, etc.

An important purpose of involvement in futurology even at

the most amateur level is that of *self-awareness*. Participation in simulation games, scenario writing, planning, helps us to see how the world got the way it is and to forecast for ourselves alternative futures. Such involvement is good "mind-blowing" technique, for it challenges our social assumptions and causes us to question the "fallout" from any particular course of action in the light of its future results. Any group or individual can try writing a scenario of its town or region, or of its schools or churches. How will they look in the year 2000? What should we be doing about it? No computers and experts are necessary to start doing futurology. It is a game any number can play, but a game which should be played in earnest.

For the church as an institution, futurology serves at least two important purposes. First of all, it *focuses attention where it belongs*—on the world and the needs of men rather than on the church and self-preservation. When one begins to look at the future, no sort of picture of the church is possible without taking into consideration all the other segments of society. In this perspective the church takes on its realistic proportion as a small postscript on the world which is called to point to God's love for his world and not to point to itself. Second, it quickly leads to the *urgency of renewal,* if not revolution, in the church today if it is going to be anything short of obsolete in the future. Short-range arguments about budgets, carpets, church schools take on a different dimension in a futurist context, and we can begin thinking about God's plan for the future and in what ways we might be faithful in participating in that plan.

EDUCATIONAL PERSPECTIVE ON THE FUTURE

We who are parents, teachers, educators, students cannot help looking at the future in educational perspective, for this is our field of application. We are interested in learning about the church, the future, theology, society in its application to *where we are* in the field of education. The White House Conference on Children and Youth may provide a way of approaching some of our own questions about planning the future. What difference does such planning make? How does it work? Will it affect the lives of those who so desperately need a good education?

Along with asking questions about our own involvement with education, we must be seeking out perspectives on the future of education. What will the schools in the future look like? Will education take place in schools, or homes, or collectives, or special interest centers? Who will control education? What values and life styles will be taught through the educational process? In what way will teaching through technology affect the budgets, planning, and procedures of schools? We must begin now to shape education which can prepare men and women to live in the future. In the view of many such as Donald Michael, author of *The Unprepared Society*, we are already too late to begin to prepare for the future. We need changes now, and those concerned with education are needed to join educational planners and politicians to work for changes.

CHURCH AND FUTURE

In talking about the future, the first concern of the church should not be its own survival as an institution. Rather, the church is called by the hope which it shares to join others in planning concrete educational and social alternatives for society. Its chief aim is not survival but a future in which men and women will be glad to live. The church is called by God's promise to face the problems and despair in the world today, confident in *his hope* for mankind:

> For I know the plans I have for you, says the Lord, plans for welfare and not for evil, to give you a future and a hope (Jeremiah 29:11).

23
FINDING
THE
PROBLEM

BY JAMES D. ANDERSON

As a young, freshly ordained priest of the Episcopal Church, I was assigned to the Sunday school, the parish education committee, and the parish high school youth group. In my position as assistant to the rector of a large congregation this assignment of responsibilities was and still is fairly normal.

Brash, eager, and too ignorant to be awed by the complexity of the task I plunged in with enthusiasm. I found a large and exciting variety of resources—teacher-training manuals, the Seabury Series (still young and growing), Dr. and Mrs. Cully in nearby Evanston, the Diocesan Education Committee—and felt invigorated by the excitement they produced. My offerings were laid before the parish education committee with the same sense of newness and I found that they, too, were infected by the vitality of our task. Only gradually did it dawn on me that I had become something of an expert in Christian education simply by my avid pursuit of the resources available. Only much later did I notice how different our parish situation was from the usual dull, lackluster educational climate of most congregations.

The situation is slightly changed today. Young clergy, fresh from their seminary training, are still being given the same type of assignment I received but I expect it meets with considerably less enthusiasm. I was recently speaking with a group of nine newly ordained clergy. Every single one of these men agreed that they found Christian education tasks to be the thing they liked doing the least. There was a chorus of agreement when one man said that he had never had an educational success and so he tended to avoid this part of his job as much as possible. One result I expect is that even fewer clergy are gaining the experience and knowledge which a careful use of the plenitude of human and multimedia resources would bring to them. The number of congregations which see their educational ministry as something akin to washday drudgery has, if anything, grown.

What is going wrong? Where is the problem? Why do parishes have such difficulty in developing effective Christian education? Why aren't parish leaders able to foster exciting visions of education for young and old and then lead people into the realization of their dreams?

First and foremost, because in general we have not known how to get at the problem. Here I need to use an analogy.

Last month I received a long-distance call from a couple who have been friends for years. The man is a doctor and they were calling to tell me that they were giving up his practice and moving to another state where the doctor would teach and consult. Part of the reason for the change is severe eye trouble, brought on in part, they felt, by the pressure and pace of his medical practice. The man's voice on the 'phone lacked its usual timbre and vitality. They told me he had been without energy, tired easily, and had been generally run down. The wife, a former nurse, commented that her husband was "systemically weak as a result of the eye infection."

When I was asked to write this article discussing what needs to happen so that a parish might break loose and dream and experiment and plan its educational ministry in ways that can potentially bring about the future they desire I was, in effect, being asked to discuss ways of diagnosing and curing a form of systemic weakness. My friend found his entire body weak, without strength and vitality because of difficulty in his eye which, in turn, had its probable origin in his style of life and work. To talk about a systemic problem is to talk about one thing leading to another in a highly complex, interdependent fashion.

A parish is a social system. The human body is a biological system. Systemically speaking, the similarities are pronounced and the analogy of my friend's illness an extremely accurate way of envisioning parish problems. No one control center manages the health of even a single part of the human body. Inscrutable and fantastically intricate are the dynamic interrelationships of the human organism with itself and its environment.

From this point of view the inability of a parish to cope educationally is a manifestation of systemic weakness, and the actual sources of the difficulty are multiple and perhaps far removed from direct educational symptoms and solutions. No one factor can be isolated and said to be the cause of educational infirmity. If the diagnosis of the problem is not approached in this manner—and it almost never is—then it is a failure of gross proportions. Most congregations have never come close to locating the sources of the infection which continue their educational failure.

I recall a congregational meeting I attended recently in which a central topic of discussion was the inadequate educational program being run for the children and teenagers. This happened to be a congregation with immense financial and people resources. In the course of the discussion the rector gave a short speech saying that he just didn't have any answers to the problem—that as he looked around the church he couldn't see any programs which might be of help to them.

FINDING THE PROBLEM

"I don't know what kind of youth program will work." As he finished this statement a woman in the congregation rose and angrily asked, "What have we ever tried?" The rector's reply was confused, evasive, and did not answer the question.

It is my experience that this brief exchange is a classic illustration of the need for a systemic diagnosis. Most of the discussion and the rector's speech assumed that the problem was how to find the proper programs.

"What is the best curriculum?"

"Do you know of an exciting model of youth programming we could try?" The energy and thrust of the conversations were devoted to a search for an answer to the question, "What kind of program will really work?" The woman's question revealed, however, that a world of far deeper and more complex issues was at stake. Her question significantly pointed to the fact that despite the unusual resources of the parish there existed a genuine inability to execute any type of new program effort. Perhaps of greater importance her question revealed the rector's blindness to an enlarged definition of the problem.

His leadership was confirming the general understanding of the problem as being one that could be solved by finding the right program idea—with the difficulty being that one just didn't seem to exist. First and foremost, the rector was unwilling to search deeply and realistically for what was really going wrong, to widen his vision to the whole parish and its environment.

I am indebted to an article published by William Pounds in the journal of the Sloan School of Management for some insight into the reasons why so many congregations have such difficulty finding the real problems that need to be addressed.[1] A problem is often defined as the difference between what is and what ought to be. In general, the process of problem finding is a process of comparing what is with some model we have for what ought to be and the difference constitutes the problem. We seem to use, in the main, three highly simplistic and naïve models for discovering discrepancies. The first model is historical. When something isn't running as well as it used to we know there is a problem, i.e., getting it to run as well as it once did. The second way we use to discover discrepancies is through other people in the organization telling us that things aren't going well. The problems we try to solve are defined by what others describe to be a problem. The third model for comparison—used far less often than the other two—is the experience of other groups and organizations. How does our performance look in relation to what others are doing is the basic question. Any one of these three methods can and does generate enough problems to consume a leader's full energies. We expend our efforts answering problems defined by:

a. How does it look in relation to what we used to do?

b. How does it look in relation to someone else's opinion?

c. How does it look in relation to another organization?

Thus, parishes use their resources answering educational problems naïvely defined as:

a. What kind of youth program will get us the same attendance we had ten years ago?

b. Parents are upset with the trouble they have getting their kids to go to Sunday school. We need a more interesting curriculum.

c. St. John's has a coffee house—maybe we need one, too.

In contrast to this form of problem definition let me describe to you the reasons given to me by the Rev. William Swing of St. Columba's parish in Washington, D.C., for their educational success. St. Columba's recently attracted my attention by building a parish education and worship event of major proportions around the idea of choreographing the music of *Joseph and His Amazing Technicolored Coat.* Because I knew this was one of a series of exciting educational experiences in the past two years I interviewed Bill to ask him why and what was making it all possible. Here is a list of Bill's reasons distilled from the interview:

1. His participation in a program of continuing education which had given him the chance to reflect on the parish.

2. The fact that the parish has used consultation help in formulating a clear set of expectations between himself and the congregation—including an emphasis on education.

3. A parish and personal willingness to sustain and utilize conflict. Dancing in the church had been quite controversial for many in this basically conservative parish.

4. A parish and personal climate respecting the feelings and points of view of others.

5. The incorporation of the parish preschool and its creative director, Sylvia Buell, more and more into the life of the parish.

6. His own willingness to become involved, to bring in others who knew more than he did, and to work hard.

7. Careful ways of inviting people to join in supporting this central thrust of parish life.

In my own experience this is a good listing of several of the interdependent factors which must be effectively present for a parish to operate in a vital educational manner. Indeed, they are some of the critical factors constituting the health or disease of the social system we call a parish. If you want some clues as to significant areas in which to look for the obstacles to creative educational work in your parish then these seven points make a good beginning. Because the list does begin to spell out the dynamic processes of parish life it is a far better model for locating discrepancies than the historical, other person, and other organization model we normally use. Issues such as the clarity of role expectations between clergy and laity or the congregation's ability to live with conflicts and to tolerate differences may seem far removed from the usual work of a parish educational committee. From the standpoint of the way things really work these are impediments precisely characteristic of parish educational failure. We can, and do far too easily, spend full time chasing solutions to problems we have not yet identified. Every parish—like every human being—is unique, mysterious, and miraculously complex. If, like the group of nine newly ordained clergy, we give up on our educational ministry in the local congregation, then we continue, I believe, to be negligent in our vocation as the people of God. Some things about a parish are understandable and the fact that, for example, a rector's role expectations can influence the quality of a parish educational program should be understandable to all of us. It is certainly as understandable as my friend's physical weakness as influenced by an eye infection as influenced by his way of life. What would we think of a doctor who did not understand and treat us systemically?

Ernest Jones in his marvelous biography of Sigmund Freud tells this story which I treasure:

> I told [Freud] once the story of a surgeon who said that if he ever reached the Eternal Throne he would come armed with a cancerous bone and ask the Almighty what he had to say about it. Freud's reply was: "If I were to find myself in a similar situation, my chief reproach to the Almighty would be that he had not given me a better brain."[2]

Freud had an insatiable desire to understand the mysteries of human life. The story indicates that rather than lamenting our human dilemma or the often inexplicable frustrations of life Freud was commending using the same energy to unravel these mysteries. I recommend this attitude to any who would seek to unravel the riddle of parish life.

24
FINDING
RESOURCES

BY D. CAMPBELL WYCKOFF

An educational curriculum program for today's local parish presents a number of acute problems. National church educational-planning bodies have begun to shy away from prescribed educational programs and have begun to offer a variety of resources from which local groups must choose. At the same time, many congregations, seeking for relevance, have decided that they must develop educational plans that are indigenous to their own needs and situations. All this seems wise but it places a new responsibility for educational planning on the local parish, a responsibility for which few are prepared. The purpose of this article, therefore, is to provide a practical aid for local churches who wish to plan their educational curriculum and program.

A CURRICULUM

Remember, a curriculum is a course to be run, a plan for encountering and dealing with meaningful, life-changing experiences. It's not textbooks, filmstrips, and other aids. These can be educational resources for a curriculum, but the curriculum is much more basic. A curriculum makes clear our goals for education and the plan or program we intend to use to arrive at these goals. That is why persons planning and carrying out educational curriculum locally need to arrive at and share common understandings of what makes their curriculum both educational and Christian.

It is important that these planners themselves be local: sharing local hopes, ideas, doubts, and questions. They must start with themselves, where they are, and gradually involve others (church officials, teachers, parents, learners) in considering these hopes, ideas, doubts, and questions. The plan must finally belong to the whole church. The curriculum must be commonly owned.

EVALUATION MAY BE A STARTING POINT

The practical impetus to localizing curriculum often comes only when we realize that we are not accomplishing what we might, when we have misgivings about the appropriateness of our present plan, or when we begin to get criticism of our present program and its results.

It is not easy to be self-critical and evaluative, to change when change seems called for, or to look at new and unfamiliar ways of doing things. But honest evaluation of what we have now and what we are now doing can get us started, and can establish a realistic base for determining the priorities and goals of our own curriculum in light of local needs and opportunities. So often churches fail in their education ministries because their programs are based upon goals and a curriculum not owned by the congregation. They also fail because these ministries are not based upon the unique situations which face a local congregation. The immediate evaluative questions, therefore, are:

Do our priorities and goals for education speak directly to the real needs of our local situation?

Do our priorities and goals take advantage of all the significant resources and opportunities in our local situation?

But the basic evaluative question is: Are we discovering and doing the will of God here and now? The starting point is God's action. When a congregation plans, that planning is a theological and biblical inquiry and enterprise. Work on our curriculum goes forward in the recognition of the fact that God is always creating something new and always requiring something new and creative of us.

LOCAL CREATIVITY AND INNOVATION

Let creative thinking and original ideas become part of the process. Don't just go by the "guidebook." The job demands individuality, creativity, and innovation from those responsible as persons, Christians, and as a church.

Make this the opportunity for getting at something you have always wanted to do—making your church's goals, curriculum, and program really fit your own situation and your understanding of the church.

A PROGRAM AND CURRICULUM COMMITTEE

The local committee on Christian education may already have as members those persons in the congregation and community who are best equipped to think through and implement the choice and development of a curriculum. If so, that committee should take on the job. If not, a special committee for this purpose should be formed. Sometimes it is best to form a new committee since there is a tendency for all of us to function according to old perceptions of the responsibility of particularly named groups. Often, Christian education committees are too caught up in the management of old programs to reflect freely on goals and a curriculum which later will be translated into a program.

"Outsiders" are also needed—community leaders, area consultants, and others. They can help with ideas and contacts, and they can help us to see how others see us and our functioning in the world.

The committee needs to provide a pattern and center of control to maintain balance in the congregation as it works out its educational mission. There is always a danger that a majority point of view or a particularly aggressive point of view may be extremely selective and bias the educational enterprise.

The committee needs diplomatic leadership. Curriculum planning can be scuttled easily if people feel that their opinions are being slighted or regarded as not important.

Complete committee records need to be kept so that as membership and committees change, what has been considered and decided will not be lost. They need to communicate continually with the total congregation so that their labors reflect the view of the church.

STEPS IN THE PROCESS OF CURRICULUM CHOICE AND/OR DEVELOPMENT

The following outline of steps in the planning process is intended to indicate how a committee might proceed to do its work and implement its decisions:

Step One: Assess your local situation both in your church and community. Attempt to establish a realistic and complete picture of the issues, problems, challenges, and opportunities that provide the setting for educational planning. What are the issues which confront your church today? In the light of those issues, what are the educational needs of your church and community? What challenges and opportunities are open to you, and what are their educational implications?

Step Two: Ask yourselves: What is the mission of our church, in our particular community, at this particular time? What are the educational goals that follow from your understanding of the church's mission? Now state the goal or goals of your church's educational program.

Step Three: Involve others in your planning process, especially those who will have responsibility for carrying out your plans (the teachers), those who are to benefit (the learners), and those who ultimately must approve your plan, your budget, and authorize its operation (the church's governing boards). Involve various segments of your congregation in providing judgments and suggestions; keep the congregation informed, especially reporting to the parents and the youth groups; seek the counsel of trained educators in your congregation and community. Seek the help of the trained, professional staff of your denomination. Attempt to construct an overall educational plan (curriculum) to meet your established goals.

Step Four: Now select particular learning experiences. In light of your decisions on the assessment of your local situation, the church's mission and its educational goals and curriculum, decide what educational experiences are needed for various persons and groups in your parish. There are two categories to consider: age levels and various functions across age levels. Take into consideration that you may not now be using the best groupings, and that new insights on essential learning experiences may give you new ideas for other groupings. Take into account that you have various options in addition to the usual ones: individually designed reading courses; groups involving a cross section of the congregation; and groups having a particular homogeneity (for example, vocation, personal or family need, response to awareness of some issue, or response to some religious movement).

With this freedom and flexibility in mind, list all the important learning experiences that you consider to be needed in your local situation for all these persons and groups for whom you are responsible according to your overall curriculum plan to meet your goals. Then check your listing against an analysis of learning experiences in Christian education such as those found in *Educational Guide, Church of the Brethren*, Appendix F, pages 85–93 (Church of the Brethren General Offices, 1451 Dundee Avenue, Elgin, Illinois 60120), or the more voluminous analysis in *The Church's Educational Ministry: A Curriculum Plan* (St. Louis: The Bethany Press, 1965). Evaluate your own list and make additions and corrections in the light of this comparison.

Step Five: Select resource materials. Use what is helpful to your individual situation. Do not feel bound to adopt more than you can use or something that does not quite fit.

Resource materials may be found in various places: traditional curriculums; reference persons (pastors, parish education workers, boards of parish education, other churches, judicatory advisers); church and public libraries (their periodicals and other media, as well as books); and denominations that are moving toward localization.

Some of the options for curriculum resources follow. These are all too brief descriptions and only meant to show the diversity of material available and not to give a fully accurate description of them or show approval or worth.

Christian Faith and Action (United Presbyterian Church in the U.S.A., Witherspoon Building, Philadelphia, Pennsylvania 19107)—Using an "inquiry" approach to learning and assuming the centrality of biblical knowledge, this graded schooling program aims at developing abilities needed for responsible participation in church and world.

The Covenant Life Curriculum (Box 1176, Richmond, Virginia 23209)—Starting sequentially with the Bible, the church, and social and personal issues as content, this curriculum aims at "activity" learning that seeks the transformation of the self by drawing people into the reality of the Christian fellowship and nurturing them in Christian faith and action.

The United Church Curriculum (1505 Race Street, Philadelphia, Pennsylvania 19102)—Using "discovery" participation method, persons are aided to respond in faith to the call of God in Jesus Christ and his church as they are helped to seek Christian solutions to life's personal and social problems.

The Christian Life Curriculum (Box 179, St. Louis, Missouri

63166)—Centering on life's concerns and the gospel, this curriculum establishes learning tasks that aim at creating an awareness of revelation, the gospel and a response in faith and love.

Beacon Series (25 Beacon Street, Boston, Massachusetts 02108)—A very innovative, diverse set of resources based upon sound educational methods and the liberal religious tradition with its concern for the living of religion.

Lutheran Church in America Curriculum (2900 Queen Lane, Philadelphia, Pennsylvania 19129)—Thoroughly research-based, with coordinated materials and guidebooks for every age and function from a primarily Lutheran perspective.

Seabury Series (815 Second Avenue, New York, New York 10017)—The Episcopal curriculum (built around the existential questions children, youth, and adults ask and reflecting upon man's experiences) is understood as only one aspect of the celebration and action in the life of a parish and its educational program. Family worship, for example, is essential.

Uniform Lessons Cooperative Series (Box 1176, Richmond, Virginia 23209)—Continues the Uniform Lessons tradition (the Bible in English in six-year cycles), and updates the educational, theological, and ethical approaches.

United Methodist Curriculum (201 Eighth Avenue, South, Nashville, Tennessee 37202)—The *Wesley Series* (two-year grading) and the *Asbury Series* (three-year grading) provide rich and flexible material for churches that want to combine traditional methods of church education with some innovative approaches.

You need to read the descriptive material which each of these publishers provides and look at some of their resources before you decide what is best for you. In every case, check their descriptions against your decisions on the church's mission, educational goals, and essential learning experiences to see what indications there are that certain materials might suit your particular local needs best.

But to go a step beyond the selection and adaptation of a total curriculum resource series, *The Educational Guide, Church of the Brethren* (Church of the Brethren, 1451 Dundee Avenue, Elgin, Illinois 60120) provides a splendid method for finding more diverse curriculum resources. This has been called "one of the most innovative resources we have." The *Guide* gives detailed directions on how to proceed to plan a locally based curriculum defined by your goals. It includes a library of resources with keysort cards, a continually updated listing of educational resources. This library of resources is a gold mine. On keysort cards are listed almost every educational resource available. In every case the resource is described, evaluated, and keyed to particular educational goals and objectives. Full information on where the resource can be purchased is provided. Once you have established your goals and curriculum plan, this provides you with a practical aid for finding the resources you might use to meet your needs. The whole process is a liberal education in the fundamentals of curriculum construction and implementation.

In any case, Step One is to establish your educational needs; Step Two, to establish your overall educational plan to meet those goals in your local situation; Step Three, to plan your diverse program for the actualization of that plan in every area of your church's life; Step Four, to secure the educational resources needed to aid in the fulfillment of your program. These four steps are basic to any church concerned for Christian education today. For further help:

DeBoer, John C., *Let's Plan, A Guide to the Planning Process for Voluntary Organizations.* Philadelphia: Pilgrim Press, 1970.

The Church's Educational Ministry: A Curriculum Plan. St. Louis: Bethany Press, 1965. Although prepared for national curriculum developers, this huge volume should be of help to local planners seriously interested in a complete, well-rounded program.

FINDING RESOURCES

The Educational Guide, Church of the Brethren. Elgin, Illinois: Church of the Brethren, 1968. A step-by-step plan for localizing program and curriculum, opening the way for completely free selection or development of materials.

Planning Curriculum Locally. Richmond, Virginia: Presbyterian Book Store (Box 1176, Richmond, Virginia 23209). Comes in two sets of directions. *Phase I* is for training presbytery and synod leaders in how to localize planning for adult education in the churches. *Phase II* takes it into the local church itself. The plan coordinates with *Lay Education in the Parish*, by Robert H. Kempes (Philadelphia: Geneva Press, 1968).

25
A NEW COURSE—
AN INTERVIEW WITH
EDWARD A. POWERS

BY JOHN H. WESTERHOFF III

(An interview with Edward A. Powers, general secretary of the Division of Christian Education of the United Church Board for Homeland Ministries)

Westerhoff: 1956 was my first year at Harvard Divinity School. I hadn't even begun to think about the church's educational ministry. But I understand that 1956 was your first year with the Division of Christian Education of the United Church Board for Homeland Ministries. Reflecting back over those fifteen years, what was going on in church education in the late 1950s?

Powers: I came to the Board from a typical parish where I had worked at a variety of mostly traditional things in church education. I found that Congregational-Christian and Evangelical-Reformed educators were engaged in a vital collaboration aimed at framing the future of Christian education. That collaboration helped shape the United Church of Christ. It was a very exciting sort of place. In a sense it was a time something like today. Once again, we are at a juncture in the life of those denominations who are committed to Joint Educational Development (J.E.D.) and striving to find a new style for future work. That same dynamic feeling was present in 1956. We were then in the period of developing a new educational curriculum. We were aware that very little innovation was going on in churches at the time. But we held a common assumption that the church in its structure and style were valid and normative. Our aim was to work on the renewal of that church. There was general agreement among the staff on the nature of education. In many ways we were probably ahead of the churches. We anticipated the significance of Jerome Bruner, Erik Erikson, and Robert Havighurst for educational theory and practice. Our educational style was much different than the funneling notion. I'm not sure we understood all the implications of what we were doing. We were involved in a much more radical educational venture than we had supposed. It was only when the curriculum began to be designed and art forms emerged that we began to get a clear picture of what we had committed ourselves to do. That curriculum, significantly consistent with the theological and educational theory we had professed, surprised us a bit. The consequences of our words were more profound than we had anticipated. In a sense the art revealed the full meaning of the intersection of faith and life we were after.

One memorable event surrounding this new curriculum was the strong reaction to a 1960 newspaper story on the nursery material that claimed we had portrayed Jesus in "clam digger shorts." The controversy seems tame by today's standards. Obviously, the debate was more than taste in art. It had to do with our understanding of the faith. It anticipated the faith crisis of today. We had shattered the stereotypes about Jesus which had made him powerless in the life of men. People had to face afresh the question of the form and meaning of Jesus. In the process, they learned something about dealing with controversy and conflict. Like today, these were exciting days.

Westerhoff: But you didn't join the staff of the Board primarily to develop that new curriculum, did you?

Powers: No, I came with the Board in a youth ministry responsibility. In fact, at first I wasn't sure I wanted to get involved in all these Christian education endeavors. They all seemed pretty narrow and parochial—even though there was a lot of excitement.

For one thing there has always been a strong tendency for Christian education to become too specialized and primarily concerned for teaching in church schools. Working on the youth beat always demanded a more holistic approach to the church and a broader understanding of education. We dealt with race and peace, with service and action, with the total life of the church and the life of youth in the community, home, and school.

Westerhoff: Were there other factors that influenced your understanding of church education?

Powers: Yes, there were. Primarily I was forced to keep a holistic perspective on education because I was a staff member of a mission board which saw Christian education in the context of mission. As only one part of that mission board, we were continually forced to see education in the context of the total life of the church and its mission.

Even as we lived in the enthusiasm of a new curriculum, we were engaged in debate by our colleagues who questioned some of our assumptions. They particularly pushed us on our assumption that if local congregations nurtured people in the faith then a faithful church would emerge. They accused us of not taking the introvertedness and cultural boundedness of the church into account.

Westerhoff: Who was right?

Powers: We both were. I still think we were right in what we set out to do then, but the critics were right too. The community of faith *does* nurture people into faith—true faith or apostasy. That's inevitable. But we were somewhat naïve about the context in which the church exists and in which the nurture takes place. We now know that we must address such problems and build a new sort of educational ministry which deals with the church's cultural captivity.

Westerhoff: What has happened since then which has influenced your understanding of Christian education?

Powers: In the past decade, the issues of war, and social and economic justice have come to our awareness as never before. We have also realized the power of corporate sin— racism is not only an individual attitude but it is incarnated in communal life and social structures. We were not as aware of that in the fifties nor did we ten years ago anticipate the whole ecumenical revolution: not only churchly unity but a new concern for the whole inhabited earth, a concern which brings us together with whole new configurations of groups and people for education in both the church and society.

Westerhoff: What's the challenge today?

Powers: We haven't yet assumed our educational responsibility as well as we might. For example, people who make war are products of Christian education programs. They learned to do that in churches. Yet it is possible to learn to deal with conflict short of war, to learn to be peacemakers, to discover how to live with diversity, to learn what it might mean to have justice for all men.

All that is part of the gospel we have taught in the past but we haven't adequately connected that message with the corporate social life of our people. We made the biblical content an end in itself and thereby divorced it from what was going on in the world. Our emphasis on content worked against us. We discovered that knowing the Bible did not necessarily make any difference in our behavior.

Our aim is the same as always: to learn Christ—that is, to learn what he was concerned about and the reality he is. We have to learn his concern for peace and justice, for the liberation of the oppressed, of freedom for all and power—the social forces and institutions which prevent persons from fulfill-ment. That means taking seriously all the experiences a person has and not just what happens in classrooms.

Westerhoff: Recently I had lunch with some anthropologists. One asked what would you eliminate in schools if you had to drop something. Another replied, "Everything except extracurricular activities." We laughed but perhaps that's where our most significant education takes place. And yet how often we cut such activities out of our schools or worse not even consider their educational importance.

Powers: That reminds me that a J.E.D. task force recently investigated sexism in two church school curricula. The findings echoed those we have on anti-Semitism. When we specifically address intergroup relations or the role of women we do pretty well. But when we are not consciously dealing with such issues we engage in anti-Semitism or sexism.

Westerhoff: How do we respond to such an awareness today?

Powers: The goal of any educational curriculum today is to look first at this hidden curriculum and make it the curriculum. In that way we will be addressing the structures which finally shape behavior and influence understanding. These are the areas of education we used to ignore and which finally crippled us. We have to see education as very contextual, environmental, experiential, and social.

For too long we used the public schools as our model. We forget that the church has an advantage. We are free from the limitations of certifying teachers or meeting academic content requirements—free, that is, to teach and live the gospel. A new and different conception of church education is possible if we use our wisdom and imagination.

Westerhoff: With that in mind, what would you say needs to be the major focus of church education today?

Powers: Shalom! The Hebrew word *shalom* has to do with more than the absence of war. It suggests well-being, community, justice, liberation, peace—the kingdom of God. In a sense it is a vision—finally a gift of God, but a gift men are called to affirm and receive.

Our concern now is to put together an educational program which takes shalom as its unifying center and then produce diverse resources to be used in numerous settings. What we need is a whole range of educational resources to help the church work at peace and justice.

With that goal in mind we are engaged in the development of a new curriculum for church education. The Shalom Curriculum is the designation we have given to this project. Initiated by the Division of Christian Education of the United Church Board for Homeland Ministries, it results from what has been learned by our past experience and our awareness of new needs. The aim of this "course to be run" is to provide stimulation, resources, and means for local churches to focus their life and educational mission on shalom, the biblical concept of peace and justice, a concept at the heart of the Christian faith.

Westerhoff: But how does this differ from our last few years' efforts?

Powers: For the last few years we have been framing our educational ministry in a response to an awareness of the acts of madness which characterize the international and racial scene. We must now build a capability to deal positively with peace and justice. We need to begin to shape a new culture.

Westerhoff: What's your prognosis for such an effort?

Powers: We need a long-range program which will involve political action decision-making, the hidden curricula, structures and institutions. We need to help frame the future rather than always respond to what is happening. These fifteen years have been very important in the history of Protestant Christian education. They will be, perhaps, best seen as the decades of transition. We are now on the brink of building a new future—an alternative future for education in the church, a new and unique effort in this century.

Westerhoff: As you consider that challenge and look at the situation in churches today, how do you feel?

Powers: I'm very hopeful. In many places, local churches· are ahead of us. All sorts of innovations exist. My greatest worry is whether we will be able to hold the church together as we struggle for a new educational ministry which is pluralistic as to form but focused upon concern for issues and the structures of society.

26
THE VISIONARY: PLANNING FOR THE FUTURE

BY JOHN H. WESTERHOFF III

Most of us are concerned about the future, but few of us feel confident that we can do very much to shape it. Many of us have dreams about a future we would like to see, but few of us believe we have the power to turn those dreams into reality. Some of us are placed in positions of leadership and decision-making, but few of us feel equipped to give the sort of leadership or make the kind of decisions which could make our hoped-for future realizable. Sometimes we try; we call it planning. But not all planning helps us to anticipate the future we desire or bring some measure of control to its formation. Often our planning only gives us the impression that we are doing something about the future. Sometimes it is even an escape from doing anything about the future at all. But nevertheless planning is in; everyone is recommending it. A multitude of people are engaged in it. About a year ago I set out to investigate some of the ways churches and Christian educators plan for church education. A number of different styles emerged. I've characterized them as follows:

1. *Annual planning.* This is the first and most typical style I observed. Those who engaged in this process rarely thought

of the future as being fundamentally different from the present. Most often bound by an annual budget, they planned one year at a time. While they attempted to look ahead, they typically responded to the inadequacies of last year's plans and the estimated needs of the coming year.

This planning process was demonstrated by a Christian education committee which, having evaluated last year's program, found that the preschoolers needed more space and the youth preferred to meet in a room where they could sit on the floor, reorganized their class space so that the preschoolers had more room and put a rug on the floor of the senior high classroom. When they thought about future needs, they found that they needed a new projector and more help for teachers. They, therefore, proceeded to raise money for the projector and convince the trustees that they should hire a part-time person to work with their teachers. They were engaged in planning and decision-making, but were not concerned for a future different from the present.

2. Social-demand planning. Sometimes planning was primarily a response to a squeaky wheel; confronted by a demand, the Christian education committee responded. Most often I discovered that those using this style of planning were locked into their present way of doing things. They did not really permit themselves to speculate about alternative purposes or goals, or alternative forms of education. They simply, within the context of their present way of doing things, attempted to oil the squeaky wheel.

For example, in one church I observed the Christian education committee had chosen to use their denomination's church school curriculum. But the teachers complained that it was too difficult to use and the parents complained their children were not learning enough about the Bible. In response to their criticisms, the Christian education committee collected a variety of curriculum resources described as Bible-centered. They let their teachers pick the one they wanted to use. That's a fairly simplistic example, but sophisticating it doesn't change the nature of social-demand planning.

3. Crisis planning. On occasion planning was primarily an attempt to escape from the most serious and obvious of a church's educational failures. That is, the Christian education committee responded to the current crisis. In fact, a great deal of what some churches were calling innovation was, at best, the piecemeal number of changes they had made in response to some crisis. Most often the future they were building resulted from dissatisfaction with the present rather than a consideration of a desired future. In the long run, crisis planning tended to result only in a new crisis.

One example I observed of crisis planning looked like this. Confronted by a rapid and sharp decline in Sunday church school attendance the Christian education committee looked for an explanation. They found that families went away for the weekends, that children complained about poor teaching and the teachers about discipline. They found other churches were confronted by the same crisis. They, therefore, began an ecumenical church school, moved their classes to a week day, hired trained teachers, and organized their school like a private school with tuition, compulsory attendance, textbooks, homework and grades. Everyone called it an innovation in church education. For the first two years the program seemed to work, but increasingly parents found it difficult to convince their children to attend and once again began to complain that the Christian education program was a failure. A new crisis had emerged out of the solution—innovation—to the old crisis.

4. Panacea planning. Some Christian education planning was based simply upon a current fad. This style of planning looked around to see what others were doing successfully; enthusiastically copy it was their answer to their educational problems. Rarely did they question whether or not the fad was worth following. This style of planning tended to shift from one enthusiasm to another but rarely had any long-range effect on building a significant program of church education. In each case, however, the committee was sure they had found their panacea.

For example, the current enthusiasm in one community was the use of sensitivity-training techniques in an open classroom church school. With one large ungraded classroom, children, youth and adults were engaged in "T" group exercises and games aimed at the development of their full human potential. As a result, this Christian education program had been rejuvenated. Almost every other Christian education committee in the area quickly moved to eliminate their present programs and copy the new exciting success they had witnessed. But in almost every case they are being confronted by numerable problems which threaten their new supposed panacea. Following the latest enthusiasm just did not seem to be wise planning, no matter how good the model.

Those are the four styles of planning I most often observed. In every case they followed the rules of "good planning." They always evaluated their current situation, established goals and objectives, prepared detailed strategies and plans of action. I concluded that it was not their method of planning but their style that was their problem. Neither annual, social-demand, crisis, or panacea planning seemed an adequate means for building an alternative future for Christian education. None, therefore, could I recommend. Committed to finding a process that could spark the planning of a dynamic and vital program of Christian education for the future, I searched on. Groping about for an alternative, I recalled an experience of a number of years before.

At the time I was participating in a number of ministerial workshops aimed at planning a new future for the church. Like most such workshops, we always began by analyzing our present needs and problems. After an hour of that, we were usually so depressed that there was no use going on. We had lost our ability to dream and we were powerless to act.

Then one weekend I was in Atlantic City—best known for its beauty contests but also known for its boardwalk. I wandered into a small concession where a crowd had gathered. The man with the mike had quite a spiel. I watched him get the crowd to give him as much as five dollars (a quarter at a time) in return for a dollar's worth of junk. Continually he hooked them on a hoped-for future gift which necessitated acting now to purchase something. They believed him, they had hope, they were able to act, they got something in return and in most every case left happily. I concluded that he might have the answer to our workshop problem.

I went back to a ministers' workshop and began with a new spiel of my own which suggested that in my pocket was all the money they needed to do anything they might wish. I told them they must have faith and take the risk or they will never know if I do or do not have my pocket full. They had nothing to lose and everything to gain. All they had to do was outline everything they hoped to do with the money. After listing their futuristic plans, I would point out to them that I had lied. I didn't have any money. But I suggested that we look at the list and see if there is still anything we might do about realizing some of their dreams without it. They most often discovered that at least half of the things listed could be done or worked on now. There was hope. They could do something. An alternative future was realizable. Why? Because they had started with a vision of what they hoped for rather than their current needs and problems.

That experience plus an introduction to the highly significant work being done at the Educational Policy Research Center at Syracuse University gave me an insight for a style of planning which could make an alternative future for Christian education possible. I've called it *Futures Planning.*

Futures planning begins with a vision of the future we hope for and only looks at the present and its problems much later. Unlike other styles of planning which begin with the present and attempt to get from that present to the future, futures planning begins with the future we desire and then looks at the present to see what has to happen in the interim so that it might be realized. Futures planning totally reverses the way we usually think about planning. It doesn't ask what is apt to be, that is a projection of the present into the future. It doesn't ask what can be, that is based entirely on an analysis of the present. It rather asks what I want it to be, that is the future I hope for.

There is more to futures planning, but let that suffice for the moment as we look at the process in detail.

Step One is scenario writing. A futures scenario attempts to describe the outline of our vision of the future without filling in all the details. It gives enough content to our vision so that we are able to plan what will need to take place for its realization and be able to recognize its germinal presence or absence as we proceed toward its actualization. Obviously there are many possible futures. The writing of a scenario helps us to clearly imagine one or more of these pictures. A futures scenario then is simply our description of the world (or small parts of it —in this case Christian education) as we imagine we would like it to be at some future time, in the case of futures planning for Christian education at least ten years hence. We use ten years or more because it frees our thinking from current demands and problems; it also gives us enough distance from the present so we can work toward its fulfillment without concern for minor setbacks and new problems or crises. A futures scenario should then be visionary—it begins in the future, but it should at the same time provide us with a plausible view of that future—one we can imagine real people living in, not a utopian fantasy. To write a futures scenario for Christian education you need to make believe you are a member of a church in the year 1982. Describe what is going on. What does the educational ministry of your church look like? Where and how is Christian education taking place and toward what end? Free yourself from the present. Sketch out your vision.

Of course each of us has his own vision. It's important in futures planning to be able to construct those personal visions so that they can be shared with others who have done the same. Therefore when you have written your scenario, discuss it with others. Push each other for clarity. Try to put your separate scenarios together. Ideally your planning group will be able to write a single composite scenario which captures all your dreams into an agreed-upon vision. If this cannot be done, write more than one group scenario. By comparing them, you will gain clarity on the issues and problems which must be resolved if you are to build an alternative future together. Perhaps compromise will be possible. Perhaps a partial agreed-upon future can be written. Strive for some sort of common vision. Once you've framed a composite scenario of the future, you are ready to move on to the next step.

Step Two. Still living in the future upon which your scenario is based, write a series of goal statements consistent with your vision. Make sure every aspect of your vision is covered by a clear, well-framed agreed-upon goal. Now take each of your goals and write a detailed description of what is going on when your goal has been achieved. This should help you check your goals against your scenario as well as gain clarity on your goal statement. When you have a clear, consistent goal statement make a list of all the positive and negative consequences you can imagine as a result of your goal being reached. Awareness of these consequences may convince you to rewrite your goal or revise your scenario. When you have your list of agreed-upon goals, prioritize them—which ones are most important to you and most likely to make your total scenario realizable. You will use only your top five priority goals in the next steps of your planning. With that list in hand, you are ready to go on to the next step.

Step Three. You now move away from the ten-years-from-now future you have been living in and come back to a date three years from the present. You are still not in the present, nor have you considered any of the problems of the present. Living in the church of three years from the present and considering each of your ten-year goals, brainstorm all the "futurible events"—that is events which if they were to have occurred by that date would contribute toward the actualization of that long-term goal—you can imagine. Now using the following criteria, evaluate these futurible events:

This is an event which:

1. Will significantly contribute to our goal;

2. Is in the future, not now existing but can be conceived of occurring three years from now;

3. Is plausible in our situation—that is, is an event you can picture taking place in your church (not some other church);

4. Has value for your church (not an event few will desire);

5. Your group can contribute to its realization (not something you have no resources for accomplishing).

Once you have some clarity on these futurible events—these three-year-from-now events—ask which three or four will together potentially move you best to your ten-year vision of an alternative future for education in the church. With these priorities established, you are ready to come back to the present and begin to establish ways of making each futurible event take place.

Step Four. This step moves you back to the present, but it still doesn't dwell on contemporary problems or concerns. It is called "force field analysis." It works like this: You take each "futurible event" and list on one side of a page all the forces which are now operating in your church which will discourage that event from taking place and all the forces operating which will encourage the event on the other. Sometimes the same force is both a discouraging and an encouraging force. In that case list them on the same line opposite each other. Now under each force draw an arrow—the length of the tail indicating the strength of the force. Examine these carefully for experience shows that you can set aside those on the discouraging side. Beware of these negatives, but concentrate on the possible, for if you reinforce and enlarge the encouraging forces your event has a good chance of occurring.

Step Five. The planning process from this point on is not unfamiliar to most of us. In the light of your encouraging forces and your futurible events, establish a behavioral objective for present action which will contribute to the actualization of that event. With this objective before you, you are ready to strategize and develop a plan of action for Christian education. Now get to work.

But in the process of strategizing your action plans, let me suggest a few rules of thumb based upon what planners have learned about innovation and change, especially in education. I'll only briefly list a few.

1. For change to take place your church needs some dissatisfaction with the way things are, some feeling of need for change or a desirable vision of what might be.

2. There exists a complex network of different groups in your church which have a stake in the change. They may desire it for many different reasons, but they all want it badly.

3. The initial change you recommended is comparatively small, makes few changes in existing program, is easy to understand and adopt.

4. There exists a "change agent" who has a supportive community and an appreciative "ear" of those in positions of decision-making.

That's futures planning. It is different from the planning I observed most Christian education committees engage in. But it's the sort of planning which I believe can make an alternative future for education in the church possible.

Obviously, my assumption and conviction is that we need to frame an alternative future. I am hopeful that it can be done, and I believe futures planning provides the means to bring it about. There is hope. We can build an alternative future for Christian education in main-line Protestant churches. Of course, it will mean learning a new style of planning. And it will take time, but it is possible. And worth it.

EPILOGUE

BY JOHN H. WESTERHOFF III

Today, the educational mission of the church is in a state of uncertainty. Professional leadership in Christian education is dwindling. Attendance at Sunday church schools continues to fall off and children drop out at earlier ages than ever before. Few parish ministers place Christian education as a high priority in their ministry. Dissatisfaction among laymen grows. The times are ripe for change. The inevitable tendency to complain about the way things are seems to be over. And here and there a new spirit is blowing, new possibilities emerging. What we need today is a coalition of dreamers and practitioners, dreamers to help us catch a new vision and practitioners to turn that vision into reality. It is a time to celebrate our uncertainty as we proceed to make new plans with a sense of tentativeness and experimentation. The signs of the times suggest that our new plans should have certain characteristics. Some have been suggested in this collection of essays, some have only been hinted at.

First, as Christian educators, we need a dramatic shift in our singular concern for the work and program of a church school to an understanding of church education which is broader than schooling. It will be increasingly essential for church educators to plan intentional programs of learning in every aspect of the church's life as well as in the homes of its members. No longer will we be able to isolate our educational program within the four walls of a church school classroom or even within the four walls of a particular church. Church education will have to acquire a broader vision of its responsibilities and be enabled to plan more comprehensive programs of church education in the future. Church educators will have to be able to help a congregation in evaluating their church as a learning and witnessing community of faith and to assist them in planning a variety of opportunities within the total life of the congregation so that it might truly introduce persons into the life and mission of the community of faith.

It will be increasingly important for the church educator to enable congregations to think and act as Christians, to become self-conscious, responsible Christians who make enlightened responses in faith, that is, to think and act responsibly as Christians to the issues which confront them and their society. The issues of peace, racial and economic and social justice will need to become the focus of action/reflection programs in Christian education. The integration of all of life and the finding of meaning in public life will need to be encouraged. A new core of leaders with such skills will have to be created for each local congregation to plan and facilitate such education. One of the crucial demands placed upon these leaders in the next few years will be that they be able to state the assumption, attitude, beliefs and values that are central to the Christian future. They need also to be able to state what the content and level of functional literacy is for the Christian. Overcoming the thought/action, intellectual/material, factual/moral separation they need to have clarity on the behaviors essential to the Christian life. Without these no one can plan significant education for the future.

Second, as Christian educators, they will increasingly need

to redirect their focus from parochial to ecumenical concerns. I am using this word ecumenical in three senses. In the first sense I am suggesting that in the future we will need to work closely together with other Protestant and Roman Catholic educators. No longer will it be possible to develop the sort of educational ministries the times require in isolation from our brothers and sisters in the faith. The second sense in which I use the word may prove more difficult for us to achieve, namely to turn Christian education into a concern with the world, the total environment, political, social, economic, man lives in. In the past we have tended to cut man off from his roots in nature and his participation in the structures of this material, political world. The word ecumenical means "the whole inhabited earth," all those forces in society which influence and shape and express the life of persons and groups.

No longer will we be able to isolate Christian education to a particular body of content—Bible and theology—or to a particular institution—the church. In the future we will need to encompass within Christian education a concept of political theology and worldly action—a vision of the inner and outer quest of man for peace, social justice, self-fulfillment, and the kingdom of God—the need to find roots in the mirror of our heritage and the power to act in the world to make it more humane. Personal conversion, nurture, and social action need to be unified in a comprehensive educational ministry.

The third sense in which I use the word may be most difficult of all for us to achieve, but it is no less important. Ecumenical education implies an understanding not only of one's own faith but the faith of other men. Increasingly, we live in the context of religious diversity. The religious life of mankind from now on will be lived in the context of religious pluralism. The problem for us all is to learn to live together not only in peace but in some sort of mutual trust, loyalty, and commitment to a new sort of world where love and justice exist for all minorities. No longer will Christian education be able to afford a singular concern for the Christian faith. The time will soon be when it will be essential for us to reintroduce the concept of religious education—not meaning the objective study of other religions but the aim of helping us all see the world not only as Christians see it but the way Buddhists, Muslims, Hindus, and others see it. The world at which we look is the same world; we need each other in a search for a new world of peace and justice. To build that kind of educational program in our churches remains the greatest challenge of the ensuing years.

To make all this possible, one other shift in our educational focus will need to emerge. We urgently need education by adults for adults to become more adult. I have claimed that we need to see education as a lifelong process. However, in the next few years we will need to turn our emphasis to adults. To prepare children for life as adult Christians is to offer children a model of the mature Christian and experiences with such mature Christians which will make possible his own growth and development into maturity. Lacking large numbers of those mature Christians in the church we will need to focus our educational effort in the direction of enabling adults to become Christian.

Well, there's my reading of the signs of the times. To a major extent this book of readings is for our interim days. It is a transition book which aims at opening up new thoughts and initiating new discussions among laymen and professionals in the church education ministry. I'm encouraged by the growing number of persons who, having accepted our contemporary challenge, have joined those of us who are chasing rainbows. To all of you I dedicate this book and close with the final note from *Values for Tomorrow's Children*:

It may appear as if I have placed a tremendously heavy responsibility on the church educator. I have! You may wonder whether everything we have discussed can possibly be accomplished. I think it can. We may have to stop some of the things we've been doing in our churches and establish some new priorities. That isn't out of the realm of the possible, if we think it important.

Like Max Lerner, I characterize myself as neither an optimist nor a pessimist, but rather a possibilist. Life is a great possibility, realizable through hope and organized, planned human activity. A birth of new vitality and relevance in religious education can break forth. It can also abort. The decision is ours. So is the responsibility.[1]

NOTES

CHAPTER 6 ON KEEPING ONE'S BALANCE
1. Taken from *Fiddler on the Roof* by Joseph Stein. © 1964 by Joseph Stein. Used by permission of Crown Publishers, Inc.
   2. E. Harris Harbison, *Christianity and History* (Princeton, N.J.: Princeton University Press, 1964), p. 22.
   3. Hans Meyerhoff, *The Philosophy of History in Our Time* (Garden City, N.Y.: Doubleday Anchor Books, 1959), p. 2. Copyright 1959 by Hans Meyerhoff.
   4. James Baldwin, "The White Man's Guilt," *Ebony*, August 1965.
   5. Gordon D. Kaufman, *Systematic Theology, A Historicist Perspective* (New York: Charles Scribner's Sons, 1968), p. ix.

CHAPTER 13 LEARNING SPACE FOR A LEARNING COMMUNITY
1. Cindy Larsen, "Child," quoted in John Larsen, "The Individual and the Learning Community," *Religious Education,* July-August 1972. Used by permission.

CHAPTER 18 VALUE EDUCATION
1. From "Under the Sway of the Great Apes" by Russell E. Baker, *The New York Times*, January 5, 1965. © 1965 by The New York Times Company. Reprinted by permission.
   2. From *Values and Teaching* by Louis E. Raths, Merrill Harmin, Sidney B. Simon. Copyright © 1966 by Charles E. Merrill Publishing Company. Used by permission of the authors.

3. From *The Harvesters: The Story of the Migrant People* by Louisa R. Shotwell, p. 39. Copyright 1961 by Louisa R. Shotwell. Used by permission of Doubleday and Company, Inc.

CHAPTER 19 A LITTLE MORE "KNOW-WHY," PLEASE
1. Portions of this article appeared in an article by the author, "Sometimes on Sunday: Reflections on Images of the Future in American Education," *Andover Newton Quarterly*, January 1972, pp. 130 f.

2. Dwight Macdonald, *Against the American Grain* (New York: Vintage Books, 1962), p. 365. Copyright 1952; © 1956 Dwight Macdonald. Used by permission of Random House, Inc.

3. I. J. Van Ness, "Sunday School Standards," *Encyclopedia of Sunday Schools and Religious Education* (New York: Thomas Nelson and Sons, 1915), III, 990.

4. John T. McFarland, "The Use of the Bell," *Encyclopedia of Sunday Schools and Religious Education*, op. cit., I, 89.

5. Henry F. May, *The End of American Innocence* (Chicago: Quadrangle Books, 1964), p. 14.

CHAPTER 21 ASKING THE RIGHT QUESTIONS
1. From *Crisis in the Classroom* by Charles E. Silberman. Copyright © 1970 by Charles E. Silberman. Reprinted by permission of Random House, Inc.

CHAPTER 23 FINDING THE PROBLEM
1. William F. Pounds, "The Process of Problem Finding," *Sloan Management Review* (Cambridge, Mass.: Massachusetts Institute of Technology, 1969), vol. 11, no. 1.

2. Excerpted from *The Life and Work of Sigmund Freud* by Ernest Jones, p. 25. Edited and abridged by Lionel Trilling and Steven Marcus. Basic Books Publishing Company, Inc. publishers, New York, 1961.

EPILOGUE—THE SIGNS OF THE TIMES
1. John H. Westerhoff III, *Values for Tomorrow's Children* (Philadelphia: Pilgrim Press, 1970), p. 109.